A RAW PERSPECTIVE

THE GREAT FEMINISM SCAM

I0095507

By

Innocent Karikoga

Published by

autonomy books

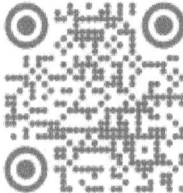

ISBN: 978–1–997657–01–9

TABLE OF CONTENTS

TABLE OF CONTENTS

Introduction

Let me say this straight:

I love women. Real women. Complicated women. Strong, soft, kind, messy, funny, stubborn, brilliant women. I love women enough to say the thing no one wants to say anymore: modern feminism is full of shit.

There. I said it. Now breathe.

What started as a necessary movement — votes, rights, dignity — got hijacked somewhere between the boardroom and BuzzFeed. Now feminism is a trademark, a personality, and a punchline, depending on who you ask. It's a product, not a principle. Liberation? You wish. It's a subscription plan with fine print: $49.99/month and your soul on auto-renew.

Feminism was supposed to make life better for women. But here's the thing — it only made it better for some. You know the type. The upper-middle-class chick with the liberal arts degree, three side hustles, and a podcast called "My Truth Is Valid". She sips overpriced oat milk lattes while railing against the patriarchy, completely unaware that the guy roasting her beans in Guatemala doesn't give a damn about her TED Talk on toxic masculinity.

Meanwhile, the single mom cleaning toilets for minimum wage? The factory worker getting harassed on the night shift? The homemaker raising three kids while being told she's "wasting her potential"? Yeah — feminism left them in the dust. Because it was never about all women. It was about getting what men had, even if what men had was stress, broken marriages, and heart attacks at 52. Equality, right?

Feminism became about copying the male struggle, not fixing it.

And now, we've got women burning out in open-plan offices, thinking this is freedom. Working like dogs to prove they're not "just moms." Free to freeze their eggs and hustle their way into existential despair. Free to cry in the shower at 32 because nobody told them that chasing a LinkedIn title might not be as fulfilling as raising a child who loves you.

Let's talk about that. Let's talk about the unspoken tax of "liberation."

You're free now, baby girl. Free to pay your rent, fix your sink, shovel your driveway in subzero temperatures because "you don't need no man." Free to work until your uterus ages out of relevance, then spend tens of thousands on IVF and call it empowerment. Free to watch your relationships crumble because men are confused, women are exhausted, and no one knows what the hell they're supposed to be anymore.

This book isn't a love letter to nostalgia. It's not a call to chain women to kitchens and pop out babies like a factory reset. I'm not here to say women shouldn't work, speak, or lead. But I am here to say we've gone completely off the rails.

We traded the prison of tradition for the prison of illusion — the illusion that endless freedom would lead to happiness. That having it "all" meant giving up everything that actually mattered.

And for the record, this isn't about hating feminism. This is about hating what it became. It became a filter. A costume. A cliquey, condescending, corporate clown show that expects women to suffer in silence if their lives don't match the Instagram version of empowerment.

You can't say you're tired. That's weak.

You can't say you want kids and a husband. That's internalized misogyny.

You can't say abortion traumatized you. That's betrayal.

You can't say you like being feminine. That's regression.

You can't say you want to be taken care of. That's anti-feminist.

You can't even say you disagree—because apparently, the "strong, independent woman" can't handle dissent.

Feminism today is not a movement. It's a cult — complete with mantras, punishments, purity tests, and excommunications.

So no, I'm not here to play nice.

I'm not writing for the applause of blue-check academics or gender studies graduates who can't make a decent meal but know over 97 genders by heart.

I'm writing for the women who got sold a lie, and the men too scared to say it out loud.

This book is a giant middle finger to the script.

To the bullshit ideas that leave women lonely, broke, overmedicated, and confused — while pretending they're empowered.

You want the truth? Here it is:

- Women still struggle. But now, they do it with less support, more shame, and louder slogans.

- Men have been told to shut up, pay up, and stay out of the way.
- And kids? They're the collateral damage of a war between ideology and reality.

I'm not here to please. I'm here to expose.

You don't have to agree with me. Hell, you probably won't.

But if something deep down inside you knows the world's lying — that something's off — this book is for you.

Welcome to the uncomfortable truth.

Take a seat and don't get too comfortable. This ride doesn't have seatbelts.

The Paycheck Illusion

The Wage Gap Lie That Launched a Thousand Hashtags

"Women make 77 cents for every dollar a man makes." Ah, yes — the feminist battle cry. Worn proudly like a badge of statistical martyrdom. Etched into HR PowerPoints, silk-screened onto crop tops, and tweeted between oat milk lattes by activists who have never heard of a peer-reviewed paper.

It's not a fact. It's a marketing slogan. A viral bumper sticker for people who confuse outrage with accuracy.

That 77 cents? It's a raw average — a number so contextless it might as well have been pulled out of a fortune cookie. It doesn't account for hours worked, job type, career gaps, education, field of study, or whether someone took a five-year detour to breastfeed two kids while blogging about their "healing journey." It's arithmetic for clowns — or worse, for people who know better and just don't care because the lie sells.

Here's a riddle: What do you get when you compare a male oil rig worker pulling 80-hour weeks in a hurricane zone to a female social media manager clocking in from her couch three days a week?

According to feminism, oppression.

According to reality: different choices, different paychecks.

But nuance is the enemy of ideology, and feminism long ago chose the easier path — victimhood with a side of influencer aesthetics.

Picture this: Ten people. One makes a buck, one makes ten, the rest are scattered in between. The average? Five bucks. Then there's another group where 10 people all make 5 bucks. Again. The average is 5. Are the two groups equal? If we give one of the people from the second group only 2 bucks, now the average of the second group is less than that of the first group. Does that mean the second group is being robbed? Nope. But if you're trying to sell a revolution, it's easier to cry "theft" than to explain math. Because math doesn't get you pity clicks. But oppression? That's *gold*.

So the 77-cent lie spreads like herpes at Coachella — irritating, hard to get rid of, and awkward to explain in public. And the people who should know better — economists, journalists, leaders — stay quiet or worse, nod along like zombies with tenure.

Because the moment you say, "Actually, when you control for lifestyle choices and time in the workforce, the wage gap pretty much vanishes," you're no longer "enlightened." You're a traitor. A sexist. A bootlicker of the patriarchy. You might as well have screamed "Make me a sandwich!" in the middle of a Women's Studies lecture.

But here's the cold truth: women aren't being robbed — they're being lied to. Lied to by an ideology that treats motherhood like a career-ending illness, and nuance like a hate crime. Lied to by movements that care more about viral slogans than actual solutions. Lied to by people who would rather sell suffering than confront the unglamorous reality that time out of the workforce matters.

Feminism doesn't want equality. It wants a villain. It needs a big, bad wolf — the evil man hoarding all the money and laughing at your unpaid emotional labour. Reality? That wolf doesn't exist. It's just your reflection in the mirror after choosing a different life path.

But hey — that doesn't fit on a tote bag.

Time, Kids, and Choices: Where the Real Gap Lives

Let's get something straight: women aren't paid less for being women — they're paid differently because life is brutal, biology is real, and choices have consequences.

You want to know where the real "pay gap" lives? It's not in some cigar-smoke-filled boardroom where men sit around plotting how to keep Becky from HR down. It's in the blood, sweat, and sleepless nights of motherhood — that ancient, unpaid, soul-draining job that feminism pretends to respect, but secretly resents.

Because feminism doesn't fight for mothers. It tolerates them. Like a drunk uncle at a wedding — part of the family, but start praying when he starts talking.

You can't climb the corporate ladder if you're too busy cleaning up puke at 3 a.m. You can't hustle for that next promotion when your toddler needs medical attention and your daycare just closed for a week because someone coughed. And you sure as hell can't compete in a cutthroat, 24/7 global economy when you've hit pause every few years to raise another human being.

And here's the kicker — nobody pays for that sacrifice. Not the company. Not the state. Not even the feminist movement that claims to be your champion. You're on your own, mama. Congratulations.

They'll march for boardroom quotas, but not for parental leave reform. They'll scream about glass ceilings while ignoring the fact that millions of women are drowning in unpaid caregiving, not because they're weak, but because they're strong enough to do what needs to be done.

But that doesn't sell. What sells is the "strong, independent, childfree career woman who don't need no man." That's the mascot of modern feminism. That's who they write articles about. That's who gets the Netflix specials, the TED talks, the CNN interviews with "lean in" platitudes and manicured feminism.

Meanwhile, the mom who left her job to raise decent human beings? She gets memes about "wasting her potential" and side-eyes at dinner parties. Because, in feminism's eyes, choosing family is failure. Choosing softness, sacrifice, or staying home means you've betrayed the cause, like you were supposed to bleed for capitalism, not childbirth.

It's sick.

We praise mothers in Hallmark cards, then toss them aside in policy.

Feminism shouts, "women can be anything," as long as it's a CEO, not a stay-at-home mom.

Feminism claims to fight for women, but only the right kind of women — the marketable ones.

So the next time you hear about the gender pay gap, ask yourself: Is it really about equality?

Or is it about punishing women who chose something different?

Feminism doesn't want to fix this problem. It created it.

Equality, But Only the Fun Parts

Feminism loves to preach about equality, but only the curated kind. The kind you can slap on a T-shirt, shout in a protest, or build a career around. The kind that demands corner offices, equal pay, and CEO quotas — but never sewer jobs, frontline combat roles, or high-risk labour. Equality is the slogan, but what they're selling is selective empowerment.

Let's be real. You want the same pay? Cool. Then, where are the marches for equal representation in oil rigs, fishing boats, and scaffolding crews? Where are the campaigns demanding that women make up 50% of the coal mining or construction workforce? Nowhere — because that kind of equality doesn't come with sponsorship deals or feminist book tours. It comes with risk, danger, dirt, and death. But modern feminism isn't interested in equality across the board. It wants parity at the top and the privilege it brings — a custom-fit version of "equal" that somehow always skips the women who bear the brunt of everyday reality of being a woman without privileges.

This movement doesn't want the same responsibilities as men. It wants the rewards men earn without the price they pay. When a man works 80-hour weeks, sacrifices family time, and takes the blame when things collapse, no one calls him empowered — they call him expendable. But when a woman makes it to the top, she's treated like a goddess who broke the system. Meanwhile, the system itself, with all its weight, risk, and failure, still rests on the shoulders of men society quietly expects to die to keep it running.

And let's not ignore how this curated version of equality treats male suffering like background noise. Suicide rates? Workplace deaths? Homelessness? Those numbers don't trend on social media. They're inconvenient truths that poke holes in the carefully polished narrative that men are the privileged class. If feminism really cared about equality, it wouldn't ignore the men who suffer quietly, break down privately, or die anonymously just to keep the machine turning.

But here's the catch — true equality is ugly. It doesn't sell. It doesn't get applause. And it sure as hell doesn't fit into a tweet. So the movement trims the fat, rebrands the struggle, and packages empowerment as a lifestyle — designer, digestible, and always conveniently incomplete.

What we're left with is not equality. It's entitlement, dressed up in the language of justice. It's a movement that wants all the upside of being male, with none of the weight. And the minute you point that out, you're not arguing — you're offending. You're dangerous. You're the enemy of progress.

But facts don't care about movements. And reality doesn't bend for slogans. The truth is: Feminists can't have equality if they're only willing to fight for the glamorous parts of it.

Feminism's Selective Sisterhood

Feminism claims to fight for all women, unless those women want a family, raise kids, or, *God forbid*, enjoy being stay-at-home moms. Suddenly, that sacred sisterhood becomes a petty mean-girl clique, and motherhood — the literal foundation of society — becomes some kind of feminist betrayal. You want to talk about internalized misogyny? Try telling a feminist you'd rather raise your children than climb a corporate ladder and watch her face twist like you just spat on Mother Teresa's grave.

The irony is painful. A movement supposedly built on "choice" turns hostile the moment your choices don't match the agenda. Feminism only uplifts women who play by the rules — chase degrees, build careers, delay kids, maybe freeze some eggs to keep up appearances

— and treat the biological clock like a nuisance instead of nature. They celebrate the woman who becomes a CEO, but mock the one who raises four kids with discipline and love. Feminism forgot its roots. It stopped fighting for dignity and started marketing a lifestyle.

And let's not pretend this is just a few loud voices on the fringe. It's baked into the cultural narrative. Movies, media, and magazine covers praise the single, childless career woman while painting the full-time mom as some outdated relic with no ambition. We've replaced feminine value with LinkedIn achievements, and call it progress. What used to be seen as nurturing and essential for humanity has been downgraded to failure, not by men, but by other women holding feminism's flag.

It's no accident. Feminism needs women to feel dissatisfied. Happy mothers raising strong families? That doesn't sell books. That doesn't fuel outrage or justify the million-dollar nonprofits built on "female empowerment." So instead, they keep the war going — not against men, but against femininity itself. Against biology. Against the natural instinct to care, nurture, and build something beyond your résumé.

And while they scream for paid maternity leave and "work-life balance," they turn their backs on the core issue: *why* isn't motherhood respected in the first place? Why is raising children — the next generation of workers, taxpayers, soldiers, voters — treated like a detour instead of a contribution? If feminism were truly about equity, it would demand that value be placed on caregiving, not shame it, not dismiss it, not bulldoze over it in the pursuit of cold, corporate prestige.

But instead, feminism leaves those women behind. The ones who don't want to "lean in," who'd rather lean into their families. The ones who give up promotions to raise children with dignity. The ones who sacrifice their bodies, careers, and sleep, not because they're weak, but because they're strong enough to carry something that matters. And for that, they're invisible in the movement that was supposed to be for *all* women.

Feminism didn't liberate women. It rebranded their worth — and sold it back to them with interest.

The Shame Machine

Once upon a time, raising a family was seen as a noble pursuit — the backbone of communities, the silent force that held entire civilizations together. Today, in the eyes of modern feminism, it's practically an act of treason. The woman who chooses family over career is no longer celebrated; she's quietly ridiculed, pitied as someone who "gave up" or "settled." Feminists love to preach that all choices are valid — but let a woman say she wants to be a full-time mother, and suddenly she's "wasting her potential," "dependent," or "brainwashed by patriarchy." The support ends the moment her choice doesn't serve the feminist brand.

Modern feminism doesn't fight for the woman who walks away from a corporate ladder to raise her children — it discards her. The single mother on antidepressants, juggling two jobs, is held up as a modern heroine, while the stay-at-home wife with a happy marriage and healthy kids is seen as an antiquated joke. There is no real "choice" here, only a performative illusion. Choose the path the movement endorses — careerism, hustle culture, and independence at all costs — and you'll be showered in hashtags and TED Talks. Choose family, stability, and interdependence, and you're on your own.

This movement has quietly turned women into economic units: billable, taxable, scalable. It doesn't care if they're fulfilled or happy — only that they're in motion, preferably in an office, generating output. A woman nurturing children, investing her time into something that doesn't show up on a GDP spreadsheet, is now seen as a liability. She's not "productive." She's not "empowered." What she is, however, is dangerous — because she exposes the lie.

When that same woman raises grounded, emotionally secure children, maintains a peaceful household, and thrives outside the system, she becomes living proof that a fulfilling life doesn't require boardrooms, business cards, or burnout. She dismantles the false narrative that the only path to empowerment is through a career. And because her life doesn't fit into the movement's pre-approved template, she must be silenced, ridiculed, or erased altogether.

The truth is harsh, but clear: feminism today doesn't serve women. It serves the machine. It's less about liberation and more about conversion — converting every woman into a working, spending, voting unit who won't rock the boat. The housewife does just that. By opting out, she reminds the rest of us that this wasn't the only road — and maybe not even the best one.

Feminism hasn't failed to support all women. It simply chose which women it wanted to elevate, and which ones it was willing to discard for the sake of a marketable message. And that choice, whether intentional or not, has cost millions of women their peace, their health, and their identity — all in the name of progress.

The Illusion That Cashed In

The wage gap isn't a civil rights crisis. It's a con. A catchy, manipulative soundbite that turned into a movement's rallying cry — not because it's true, but because it's *useful*. It turns every spreadsheet into a battlefield, every paycheck into proof of patriarchal oppression. And the worst part? People bought it. Hook, line, and pink tax.

But this illusion came at a cost — not to men, but to women. Real women. The kind who don't see their lives as marketing campaigns. The mothers. The caregivers. The ones who said no to the soul-sucking grind and yes to something bigger than themselves. Feminism told them they were failing, and did nothing to fight for the value they create.

Instead of tackling the real problem — how society punishes women for raising the next generation — feminism took a shortcut. It blamed men, simplified the math, slapped it on a tote bag, and called it empowerment. Meanwhile, women who veered off the corporate path were quietly erased from the story. Not sexy enough for the movement. Not profitable enough for the brand.

So here we are — a culture obsessed with pretending that women are powerless victims of evil boardrooms and cigar-smoking executives, when in reality, the deeper injustice is how little we respect the work that *isn't* done in suits. Feminism chant "equal pay" while turning their backs on the unpaid labour that keeps the whole damn system alive.

The truth? The wage gap isn't proof that the system hates women — it's proof that the system doesn't know how to measure value unless it comes with a salary attached. And feminism, for all its noise, made that problem worse. Not by fighting too hard, but by fighting for the wrong damn things.

Next time you hear "77 cents on the dollar," don't get mad. Just laugh. Then ask them if they've ever raised a child, wiped a fevered forehead at 3 a.m., or sacrificed ten years of momentum to give life to another human being. Because *that's* work. That's value. And if feminism can't see it, maybe it's time we stop listening to feminism.

You Can Be Anything — Except a Mom

Fertility Is Collapsing — And Nobody Cares

We are witnessing a quiet extinction. Birth rates across the developed world aren't just falling — they are imploding. Entire nations are on the path to demographic suicide. Japan is already in freefall. South Korea has the lowest fertility rate ever recorded. Europe is hollowing out from within. The West is aging, shrinking, and cracking — and nobody is hitting the brakes.

This isn't a distant problem for "the future." It's already here. Schools are closing due to a lack of students. Pension systems are gasping under the weight of retirees. Whole towns are turning into ghost shells, populated by the elderly and the lonely. And yet — silence. No marches. No hashtags. No emergency task forces. Because, unlike climate change or wage gaps, the death of a civilization through childlessness doesn't fit neatly on a protest sign.

Why? Because acknowledging the crisis would require confronting the ideological machinery that helped create it.

That's where feminism comes in.

For decades, feminism has championed "choice" — but only the right kind of choice. Want to delay motherhood for a corner office? Brave. Want to freeze your eggs and outsource childcare to a stranger so you can chase quarterly bonuses? Empowered. But say you want to marry young and raise kids while your body is most fertile — suddenly you're a disappointment, a sellout, a brainwashed pick-me.

Feminism promised women freedom, but delivered them a trap: chase the same success metrics as men or be dismissed as backwards. It wasn't enough to have access to education or work. No, real worth now came only through relentless productivity. Motherhood? That was rebranded as failure. Dependence. Weakness. A betrayal of the movement. Women weren't just encouraged to postpone family — they were socially punished for prioritizing it.

Meanwhile, the system made good on feminism's betrayal. Wages stagnated. Housing prices exploded. Dual incomes became a necessity, not a luxury. One-income households, once the norm, became unsustainable. Motherhood went from being a natural life stage to an economic liability.

The state responded, not by supporting families, but by subsidizing single motherhood and dependency, reinforcing a broken cycle. Feminists didn't protest. They didn't call for tax breaks for married parents or subsidized daycare, or maternity protections. They cheered the collapse as a win for female autonomy. They sold the story that women don't need men, that family is optional, and that children are just another consumer choice, like buying overpriced yoga pants or getting a tattoo.

But the lie is bleeding us out.

Women are more "empowered" than ever, yet more medicated, more depressed, more alone. Fertility clinics are booming while maternity wards are shutting down. Feminism tells women they can be anything, but forgets to say at what cost. It weaponized freedom against nature. It told women to race the clock, beat biology, and come out smiling. Now it's all egg-freezing regret forums, fertility influencers, and late-night sob sessions for the dream that was traded for a cubicle and a cat.

A civilization that teaches its daughters to fear motherhood is a civilization that will not survive. But feminism, in its current form, doesn't care. It has no answers for this collapse. Because it *caused* it. Because its high priests measure equality in board seats, not birth certificates. And by the time they realize what's missing, there will be no one left to listen.

This isn't progress. It's slow death with a glossy PR campaign.

Motherhood: The Most Expensive Unpaid Job on Earth

There was a time, not long ago, when a single income could sustain a family. One man's salary. A roof, meals, maybe even a vacation. It wasn't glamorous, but it worked. Families survived. Children had stability. Mothers had the time and space to do the hardest job on earth: raise human beings.

Now? That life is a fairy tale. Today, a woman who chooses to stay home with her children is treated like a financial liability — or worse, a lazy dependent. She's not praised, not supported. She's punished. With economic vulnerability. With social invisibility. With a mountain of bills and no income to cover them.

Motherhood has become the most expensive unpaid job on earth. No salary. No pension. No promotions. No annual review to reward your 3 a.m. diaper blowouts or your trauma-soaked calls from the pediatric ER. Just stretch marks, postpartum depression pamphlets, and a tax credit that sometimes doesn't even cover diapers.

Meanwhile, what do we celebrate? PowerPoints. Marketing plans. DEI initiatives. We hand out plaques and six-figure salaries for women who've "made it" in corporate spaces, while mothers are sidelined, mocked, or quietly erased. Our culture holds networking brunches for childless executives while moms are told to hustle harder or quietly accept their reduced status in the social hierarchy.

And feminism? The movement that claims to speak for all women? Nowhere to be found. Unless, of course, you're climbing the corporate ladder. Then feminism will write think pieces in your honour. But if you dare to say your dream is to be a mother — a full-time, stay-at-home, raise-my-kids-with-my-own-hands mother — suddenly, you're the problem. A traitor. A woman who "settled."

It's no accident. Modern feminism doesn't support women. It supports *a type* of woman — the one who behaves like a man, earns like a man, competes like a man, and reproduces only if she can do it without disrupting her LinkedIn trajectory. The rest? Ignored. Dismissed. Shamed.

Women were sold a lie: that "having it all" meant doing it all. Work like you don't have kids. Raise kids like you don't have work. Collapse in private. Smile in public. And if you burn out? If your marriage fails? If your kids struggle while you chase endless meetings and deadlines? That's the system's fault, and not yours.

But here's the truth: mothers are the backbone of civilization. They raise the next generation. They carry the weight of emotional labour, discipline, guidance, and sacrifice — all without pay. All without prestige. They do the invisible, gruelling work that no economy can function without.

And feminism? It hasn't just failed to support mothers. It has *abandoned* them. It took the most sacred role a woman can choose and reduced it to a punchline in a TED Talk about "wasted potential."

We don't just have a fertility crisis. We have a values crisis. A culture that treats motherhood like a failure, like a plan B, is a culture sprinting toward collapse.

And unless we start to value mothers with more than patronizing Instagram posts and lip service, we'll pay the price in ways no GDP graph can measure.

Government Aid That Traps, Not Liberates

Let's talk about the so-called safety net. Welfare. Assistance. Social support. On paper, these programs exist to help women, particularly single mothers, survive. In some cases, they do. For the most vulnerable, these supports can be lifesaving. But more often, what's marketed as compassion is actually containment. A velvet cage. A system designed not to elevate, but to pacify.

Because the truth is harsh: the current aid model traps more women than it frees. It is structured to reward instability and punish ambition. Want to get a better job? You risk losing your benefits. Want to marry the father of your child? You might lose housing support or food stamps. Want to pursue education or training? Good luck navigating the red tape. The system dangles just enough to keep you compliant, but never enough to let you climb out.

These programs, in their current form, don't empower mothers. They *domesticate* them — politically, economically, and socially. And behind the bureaucratic language of "eligibility" and "means-testing" lies a brutal reality: the state is subsidizing fatherless homes while quietly discouraging the formation of stable families. It's not just negligence. It's policy.

And feminism? The self-declared champion of women's rights? Nowhere to be found.

In fact, it's worse than silence. Feminism has aligned itself with this broken structure. It has rebranded dependency as empowerment, and struggle as strength. It celebrates the single mother who "does it all" while ignoring that she never wanted to do it alone, and shouldn't have had to. It repeats the mantra "you don't need a man" like a gospel, never admitting that it's the state that steps in when the man is gone, and that dependency merely shifts from one man to another.

Feminism has become a co-author of this new arrangement: marriage replaced with government oversight, fatherhood substituted with bureaucrats, and true autonomy swapped for a lifetime of managed poverty.

And the cost isn't just economic. It's generational. Children raised in homes ensnared by these systems often inherit the same struggles. The cycle tightens. A mother raises her child under the weight of scarcity, with limited mobility, and no real exit. That child grows up learning how to survive, not how to thrive. Welfare becomes a family tradition, not a temporary solution.

The state has made motherhood bureaucratic and survivalistic — something to be tolerated, not honoured. And feminism, instead of screaming from the rooftops, has chosen to applaud the struggle. As if pain equals progress. As if mothers should wear their exhaustion as a badge of honour rather than a cry for help.

If feminism truly cared about women, it would be lobbying for systems that *lift* mothers, not just sustain their dependency. It would fight for policies that make family formation viable, that make marriage rewarding instead of risky, and that respect motherhood as a civic contribution worthy of serious investment.

But that's not the feminism we got.

We got a feminism that preaches liberation but partners with the state to control women's choices. A feminism that punishes women for choosing family over career, and cheers when they become wards of the welfare system, as long as they do it with defiant hashtags and a sense of corporate-aligned "empowerment."

Motherhood, under this model, becomes less a calling and more a cautionary tale.

And the government? It's not your co-parent. It's your captor with a smile.

The Corporate Lie Sold to Women

Modern feminism didn't just overlook motherhood — it vilified it.

Somewhere along the way, the movement stopped being about choice and started being about conformity. Not to tradition, but to capitalism. The ideal woman was no longer a mother raising the next generation with care, strength, and sacrifice. She became a sanitized corporate avatar — power suit, iced coffee, back-to-back meetings, KPIs instead of lullabies.

This wasn't empowerment. It was conscription.

Women were told the boardroom was the battleground for equality. That climbing the corporate ladder — no matter how gruelling, isolating, or soul-numbing — was the highest form of liberation. They were taught to chase titles, not toddlers. To aim for quarterly profits, not healthy families. And if they dared to want something different — a life centred around home, children, or community — they were accused of "holding women back."

Feminism, the very movement that once fought for dignity and autonomy, became the loudest cheerleader for a system that treats people, especially women, as human resources. The irony is brutal: in rebelling against the domestic sphere once framed as a "prison," feminism marched women straight into another — one with fluorescent lights, unpaid overtime, and anti-depressants tucked discreetly in desk drawers.

Let's be honest: most women working those 80-hour weeks aren't chasing a dream. They're trying to survive. They're managing stress, fertility, dating, and debt — all while pretending they're "thriving." And when burnout hits, they're gaslit into thinking the problem is them. They just need to lean in harder. Meditate. Get a better planner. Never mind the fact that the whole system was never built to nurture real human lives — only productivity.

Meanwhile, the one role that ensures civilization continues — *motherhood* — is sidelined, sneered at, and stripped of value. It's branded as regressive, lazy, or low-status. The most vital job in society — raising the next generation — has become the most thankless.

Because in the new feminist orthodoxy, being a corporate employee is seen as "strong," but being a mother is "settling." Building wealth for shareholders earns applause. Building a family earns suspicion. The woman who sacrifices her youth and health to birth and raise a child is asked, "But what do you *do* all day?" The woman who spends ten hours formatting a slide deck is praised as a go-getter.

This isn't equality. This is exploitation with better branding.

True liberation would mean giving women the real freedom to choose, without punishment, ridicule, or financial ruin. But we don't have that. What we have is a system that forces most women to work like men, live like machines, and parent like part-timers. All while pretending that this is progress.

Feminism's fatal flaw was its failure to distinguish between liberation and assimilation. Rather than creating space for women to define success on their own terms, including in the home, it simply shoved them into the mould men had already broken under.

And in doing so, it betrayed the very women it claimed to empower.

Because the truth is: working for a faceless corporation, grinding out deliverables for someone else's legacy, isn't liberation. It's just wage slavery with a LinkedIn profile.

And feminism helped sell it.

Feminism's Selective Advocacy

Feminism today loves a headline — but only when it flatters the narrative. If a woman is climbing the corporate ladder, breaking glass ceilings, or starting a six-figure business, the movement will hoist her up like a war hero. Media coverage. Hashtags. Think pieces. Applause.

But if a woman opts out of the rat race — if she says, "*I just want to be a mom,*" — the reaction is starkly different.

She's met with silence. Or worse, sarcasm. Mockery. Smirking labels like "pick-me." She's painted as brainwashed, unambitious, or complicit in patriarchy. The message is clear: feminism supports women, but only the right *kind* of women — the ones who toe the ideological line. Not the ones who bake bread, raise children, or find joy in the domestic.

This is where feminism stops being a belief and starts being a brand. A curated, marketable identity sold through slogans and TED Talks. It thrives on visibility, not nuance. It doesn't ask *what* a woman wants — only *how* her choices serve the movement's image. If your life looks good on Instagram, in a pantsuit, holding a "Boss Babe" mug, you're celebrated. But if it looks like morning sickness, nursery rhymes, and sacrifice? You're either invisible or a punchline.

This is not empowerment. This is propaganda with pink tank tops.

Feminism claims to champion *choice*, but what it promotes is conformity. It doesn't fight for women to live freely; it pressures them to live identically. And in that process, it silences the millions of women whose dreams have nothing to do with corner offices or corporate performance reviews.

This selective advocacy doesn't just fail to support mothers — it actively erases them.

Where are the marches for stay-at-home moms who get no pension, no prestige, and no peace? Where are the rallies for the women choosing family over hustle? They're nowhere, because those women don't fit the brand. They don't generate viral content or clever merch. They're not marketable.

Feminism's dirty little secret is this: it doesn't care what empowers *you*. It only cares what empowers *it*. It doesn't uplift *all* women. It uplifts the women who can be weaponized to push an agenda, one that is increasingly indistinguishable from corporate consumerism.

Real feminism means standing with *every* woman, not just the ones making headlines.

Until feminism can celebrate a mother with the same enthusiasm it does a CEO, it will remain what it has become: a movement more obsessed with optics than outcomes, and more devoted to status than sisterhood.

Motherhood — the most fundamental act of human survival — has become the greatest casualty of modern feminism's failure. While the movement screams about equality, it quietly sidelines the women who keep society alive: the mothers. They're the ones who bear the physical, emotional, and financial cost of reproduction, yet they're treated like second-class citizens in the economy and culture.

Feminism promised liberation, but for mothers, what it delivered was invisibility and indifference. No meaningful policies for affordable childcare, no extended maternity leave that works, no real economic support that values the work of raising the next generation. Instead, the narrative pushes women into corporate rat races and glorifies careerism as the only path to fulfillment, as if chasing KPIs and climbing ladders is the ultimate freedom, and motherhood is a sign of weakness or failure.

The state's so-called "help" often traps single mothers in a vicious cycle of poverty and dependency. Welfare programs, while well-intended, have become velvet handcuffs that punish stability and disincentivize marriage. Yet feminism stands silent, parroting the lie that women don't need men and should celebrate independence, even when that independence is funded by government checks and leaves women isolated.

The result is a society with plummeting birth rates, fractured families, and millions of women stuck between impossible choices: chase a career and sacrifice family, or choose motherhood and face economic hardship and social scorn. Feminism's selective advocacy means it applauds the woman who breaks the glass ceiling but mocks the one who breaks the glass cage. This isn't liberation — it's a one-dimensional brand that prioritizes clicks, slogans, and corporate careers over the messy, vital reality of women's lives.

If feminism truly wants to be a movement for women's freedom, it must expand its definition of success. It must demand policies that support all women — the career climbers, the mothers, the single parents — with real economic tools, social respect, and cultural recognition. Until then, feminism risks becoming not a force of empowerment, but a new cage, one that shackles women to an ideal that serves markets and ideologies more than actual human needs.

The real revolution won't come from hashtag campaigns or boardroom selfies. It will come from facing the uncomfortable truth: motherhood is hard, expensive, and underappreciated. It's the most important job on earth, and until it's treated like one, our society is headed for collapse.

And feminism? It can either wake up and fight for the women who keep the world turning — or it can watch as its relevance fades alongside the families it left behind.

Fixing the Math

A Radical Idea That's Long Overdue

If we want a future, we need babies. If we want babies, we need mothers. And if we want mothers, we need to stop punishing them — economically, socially, and culturally — for choosing to reproduce.

It's astonishing that in the 21st century, the one act that sustains civilization — bringing life into the world — is still treated as a personal indulgence instead of a national necessity. No nation can survive, let alone thrive, without a steady stream of new citizens. And yet, we continue to make motherhood the most thankless, unpaid, unsupported labour imaginable.

It doesn't have to be this way.

Here's a bold but practical solution:

- A permanent 25% income tax reduction for every biological child a woman has.
- This benefit is fully transferable to her spouse if she chooses not to work, allowing the household to benefit regardless of which partner stays home.
- For adopted children, a 12.5% lifelong tax break per child, to honour the profound commitment

of raising a child not born of one's body, but still very much one's responsibility.

And to make this policy fiscally responsible and resistant to abuse, the tax break would apply to household income up to a certain maximum, like the country's median income. Earnings above that threshold would be taxed as normal. This ensures that working- and middle-class families, the demographic most affected by the financial burden of raising children, are supported without turning the policy into a windfall for the ultra-wealthy.

This isn't about bribing women to have children. It's not about social engineering or imposing values. It's about acknowledging the obvious: that raising children is valuable work. That it benefits everyone, even those who choose not to have kids. And that, right now, the system makes it financially suicidal for many women to even consider it.

Ask any mother what having a child does to her career, her income, her body, her time, her mental health — and you'll hear stories of sacrifice that don't end after maternity leave. These are not temporary inconveniences. They are long-term consequences that ripple across a woman's entire working life. Lost promotions. Gaps in the résumé. Penalties for flexibility. Childcare costs that eclipse entire paychecks.

And what do we give in return? A paltry child tax credit. Maybe subsidized daycare — if she's lucky. And endless lip service from politicians and feminist figureheads who claim to champion "women's choices," as long as those choices align with careers, not cribs.

This proposal flips that equation. It tells women: you are not disposable, and your contributions at home are not invisible. You're not less ambitious for choosing motherhood. You're not a burden to the system — you *are* the system. You are the reason there's a future workforce, a future tax base, a future country.

By making motherhood economically viable, we open up choices for women. Real choices. Not just between career and children, but the ability to pursue both, or either, without being punished either way.

This policy could even help reform the welfare system. Many single mothers who currently rely on government assistance would find it easier to re-enter the workforce if they knew a significant chunk of their income wouldn't be taxed. This could reduce dependency on state aid, encourage family stability, and foster economic participation among those currently trapped in the poverty cycle.

Feminism, for all its talk of liberation, has never proposed anything this concrete — and that's telling.

Perhaps because acknowledging motherhood as valuable labour forces the movement to admit that women are not just men with different plumbing. That biology matters. That choices come with costs. That gender equality doesn't mean pretending reproduction is irrelevant.

This isn't about giving women more than men. It's about giving them back what they've already paid — in their bodies, in their time, in their earning potential.

Let's do the math. A woman who has four children by 30, and begins her career in earnest at 40, could still work 30–40 years. That's not some fringe case — that's reality for millions. And yet we act as if any break from the workforce renders her useless. With a policy like this, she can build wealth, invest in her future, and regain professional ground without being penalized for having done the most difficult and important work of all.

Is this a perfect plan? No. But it's a starting point. And compared to the ideological gymnastics feminism has performed to avoid uplifting motherhood, this is a plan rooted in both compassion and common sense.

If we want women to have children — and we do, because without them, everything collapses — then it's time we started acting like it. This policy wouldn't just fix the math. It will restore the dignity of motherhood.

The Economic Logic of Reproduction

You don't need to be an economist to grasp this fundamental truth: a society that doesn't reproduce is a society in decline. No matter how advanced, wealthy, or progressive a country becomes, it cannot outsmart demographics. Fewer births mean fewer workers. Fewer workers mean fewer taxpayers. Fewer taxpayers mean shrinking pensions, underfunded healthcare, and crumbling infrastructure. Eventually, no one is left to maintain the very institutions we once took for granted.

Every nation, whether it admits it or not, depends on one thing above all: people. Human capital is the foundation of economic growth, innovation, military readiness, and national sustainability. And yet, the act that brings people into the world — motherhood — is often dismissed as a personal choice, no more consequential than a hobby like knitting or yoga.

This cultural attitude is not just disrespectful. It's economically suicidal.

Every child born and raised into a functioning, productive adult contributes significantly to the nation's wealth and production. They grow up to become engineers, teachers, entrepreneurs, mechanics, soldiers, nurses, and Uber drivers. They start businesses, buy homes, pay into pension systems, and fund the social services that sustain others. A single well-raised child contributes millions in lifetime economic output. Yet the entire cost of creating that economic asset — from pregnancy to preschool to university — is largely borne by the mother (and often the family), with little more than token government support.

This is backward economics.

No business survives by punishing its suppliers. No country survives by punishing its mothers.

And that's where the reproductive tax policy comes in — not as a handout, but as a long-overdue realignment of incentives. A 25% permanent tax reduction per biological child — transferable to a spouse in households where one parent stays home — isn't a luxury or a loophole. It's a national investment in the single most important resource we have: people.

For adopted children, a 12.5% tax break recognizes the immense social value of caring for children already born, giving them stable homes and long-term futures. Adoption is no less a service to society, and those who step up to take on that responsibility deserve to be treated as contributors, not charity cases.

This policy is not about compulsion. No one is forcing anyone to have children. What it does is respect the economic value of those who do. It shifts motherhood from being a penalty on earning potential to a legitimate form of contribution — one that's rewarded, not punished.

Critics may say, "Well, why should people without children have to pay for this?" The answer is simple: you already do — and you always will. Every hospital, road, pension, and government program you benefit from today is funded by the taxes of someone else's child. If you plan to retire, you're counting on a future workforce that will feed, clothe, house, and care for you. And unless we start replenishing that workforce, your golden years will be anything but golden.

We are already seeing the warning signs. Countries across Europe and Asia are shrinking. Japan's population is in freefall. South Korea has the lowest birthrate in the world. Canada and the United States are watching their native-born populations plateau or decline. Immigration, while helpful, cannot solve everything, and without births, even immigrants become a finite solution.

This policy does not seek to micromanage reproduction. It seeks to restore the dignity and financial viability of motherhood. It says: yes, you are doing something valuable. Yes, we see you. And yes, your choice to create life helps keep the country alive.

A mother should not have to choose between a child and a career, between stability and sacrifice. A child should not represent a financial cliff for the family. And a nation should not pretend that demographics are someone else's problem.

This tax break is not just fair — it's vital. It's the economic acknowledgment of something we've known deep down all along: that no country survives without women who are willing to give birth, and no future is possible without the people they raise.

Feminism's Great Blind Spot

Modern feminism, at least in its mainstream incarnation, has a curious fixation: it wants to see more women in corporate boardrooms, political offices, and CEO positions — and that's where the conversation usually ends. The symbol of success is always upward mobility in career terms. Prestige. Power. Visibility. But when was the last time feminism fought — really fought — for the woman who chose to stay home and raise her children?

The truth is uncomfortable: modern feminism has turned its back on motherhood.

It claims to be about "choice," but it only validates certain choices. A woman who delays childbirth to climb the corporate ladder is "empowered." A woman who hustles for a promotion or starts her own business is "strong." But a woman who chooses to stay home and raise her children full-time? She's seen as wasting her potential. Settling. Even betraying the movement.

That's not liberation. That's a new form of elitism — one that dismisses the most natural and essential role a woman can choose not because it lacks value, but because it lacks prestige.

The global feminist agenda has poured billions into programs that push girls toward STEM fields, female leadership initiatives, gender quotas in boardrooms, and campaigns to close wage gaps. But where is the movement for mothers? Where is the investment in making parenthood sustainable? Where is the advocacy for tax relief, workplace flexibility, or long-term compensation for the economic sacrifices women make to bring life into the world?

Nowhere.

Because motherhood doesn't fit the script.

And heaven forbid someone suggests that being a mother might matter more than being a manager.

There are no Nobel Prizes for parenting. No Time Magazine "Mother of the Year" covers. No panels at Davos discussing the macroeconomic importance of stay-at-home parents. And certainly no calls from the United Nations for global motherhood recognition policies. It's as though the entire machinery of progress has decided that the labour done inside the home — unpaid, unglamorous, and often invisible — doesn't count.

But here's the irony: society cannot function without it.

A manager can be replaced. So can a consultant, an accountant, or a programmer. But a mother? A child only gets one. And for the first critical years of life, no system or salary can substitute for what a devoted mother provides.

It's not anti-feminist to say this. In fact, a truly feminist movement would be screaming about it from the rooftops.

Because if feminism is about empowering women to choose their own paths — and not just chase male-defined success — then motherhood deserves to be respected, funded, and protected as much as any other pursuit.

This tax proposal isn't an attack on women's careers. It's an acknowledgment that the freedom to choose family is just as valid, just as feminist, and just as worthy of structural support as any boardroom promotion.

Until feminism embraces this truth, it will remain blind to the one domain where women hold unmatched power — and to the one role that no man can ever truly replicate.

Tax Incentives as True Empowerment

This proposal isn't just policy — it's a paradigm shift.

A 25% lifelong tax break per biological child (12.5% for adopted) does what no feminist policy has ever managed to do: it gives women real power to choose. Not symbolic power. Not motivational speeches. Not grants for boardroom seminars. Actual financial empowerment.

For decades, the feminist movement has championed the idea of choice — but only within a narrow, sanitized frame: choose to work, choose to climb, choose to shatter glass ceilings. But what about choosing to raise a family? What about choosing to step back from a career — or never start one — in order to raise the next generation of citizens?

That choice has been economically punished for too long. This tax policy begins to correct that injustice.

With a lifelong 25% tax break per child, women can finally make decisions about family and career without fear of financial devastation. It provides mothers with the rarest form of liberty in modern society: economic breathing room. The ability to pause, plan, and prioritize the human beings they've brought into the world, without being penalized for it by the tax code.

It also acknowledges a truth society has long tried to ignore: motherhood is labour.

Not just emotional labour, but real, measurable, GDP-influencing labour. Childcare, nurturing, education, and healthcare coordination — this is unpaid work that keeps the country running and the economy afloat. It's high-skill, high-impact, and often thankless. And until now, it has been systematically excluded from any meaningful form of compensation.

So, yes — some women will end up making more than men under this plan. And that's fine. Because this policy isn't about flipping power structures or settling scores. It's not about revenge or quotas. It's about fairness. It's about finally recognizing the human engine that keeps civilization alive and functioning.

But here's something else feminism never dared to admit: this might be the best anti-poverty, anti-welfare strategy we've ever had.

How many women stay on welfare not because they want to, but because the math doesn't work any other way? With childcare costs rising and tax rates gutting their paychecks, working outside the home simply doesn't add up. But if a mother knew she could work and keep more of her earnings, she might finally see employment as the better option, not just financially, but in terms of dignity, purpose, and independence.

That's what real empowerment looks like.

A policy that respects both work and motherhood. That values both income and sacrifice. That lifts women, not by pushing them into corporate moulds, but by acknowledging their full range of contributions — public and private, paid and unpaid.

In a world where feminism continues to pretend that freedom is only found in offices and boardrooms, this proposal dares to say: freedom can also live in the home — if we choose to fund it.

It's Not a Handout — It's a Thank You

Critics will roll their eyes. They'll call it outdated. Regressive. A handout for breeders. They'll say this tax break coddles women, reinforces "traditional gender roles," and drags us back to the 1950s.

But let's call that what it is: cowardice wrapped in ideology.

This isn't a handout. It's a thank you. It's the bare minimum a civilized society should offer the women who make its very existence possible. A mother gives everything — her body, mental health, physical wellbeing, earning potential, time, sleep, and often her future — to create and nurture the next generation. She sacrifices in silence, and she does it while paying taxes into a system that gives her nothing in return.

This policy says: We see you. We value you. And we're done letting you shoulder the nation's survival alone.

It's not a freebie. It's not charity. It's compensation for a vital service — one that underpins every other sector of society. There would be no economy without mothers. No schools. No hospitals. No pensions. No police. No soldiers. No taxpayers. No future.

To call this proposal radical is to admit how little we've done for mothers until now. It's only "controversial" because we've built an entire economic system on the unpaid labour of women, and we're afraid to confront that truth.

This is a sane, practical, economically sound response to an existential crisis. Birth rates across the West are falling below replacement levels. And despite all our talk of equality and empowerment, we've created a system where starting a family is a financial death sentence — especially for women. We obsess over getting more women into tech, into politics, into STEM, while completely ignoring the fact that fewer and fewer women are choosing to become mothers at all.

And why would they? We've made it nearly impossible. We tell them to wait, to work, to "have it all," and then we punish them when they try. We push them into workforce models designed for single men in the 1950s, and then we pretend it's progress.

This tax incentive doesn't take us backward. It's the first real step forward — a policy that aligns economic priorities with demographic realities. A policy that says mothers matter. Not as symbols. Not as tokens. But as citizens who deserve compensation for the work they already do.

And yes, some will still scream that it's "unfair" — especially to the childless.

But here's the hard truth: those without children are subsidized by those who raise them. Every doctor, teacher, plumber, or taxpayer who keeps society functioning tomorrow will come from the womb of a woman who bore the costs — financially, physically, emotionally — without asking anyone else to step in. All this policy does is balance the scale.

If anything, we're late. This isn't utopia. It's triage.

And it's about time.

A Future Worth Building

Now imagine this woman enjoying a lifetime of tax relief — a recognition that her work didn't start with her first paycheck, but with her first child.

That's not exploitation. That's justice. That's foresight. That's an investment.

We call this tax policy generous, but maybe we've had it backward all along. Maybe what's truly generous is the woman who gives her prime years, her sleep, her career trajectory, and often her health, to ensure the nation doesn't fall off a demographic cliff. Maybe what's generous is the mother who raises four taxpaying citizens while being taxed into oblivion herself.

She raised citizens. She deserves that break.

And even if you never have children, even if you don't like children, you benefit. You benefit from the doctors who treat you, the plumbers who fix your broken pipes, the engineers who keep your bridges standing, and the nurses who hold your hand at the end of your life. None of them got here without a mother. And most of those mothers paid the price alone.

So, no — this isn't some fringe proposal. It's not utopian. It's not a bribe. It's not an attack on feminism or on women who choose careers over children. It's a plan for survival — practical, just, and long overdue.

Because the truth is this: a country without babies has no future. No economy. No social safety net. No innovation. No defence. No civilization. Full stop.

And to those who still think this is about "taking us back," ask yourself: back to what? A time when women's work in the home was invisible, uncounted, and unpaid? That's not nostalgia — that's the current system.

This proposal corrects that. It says motherhood isn't just a personal choice — it's a national contribution. And those who make it deserve more than just flowers on Mother's Day.

To the feminists still fighting for more women in boardrooms while ignoring the empty nurseries and collapsing birth rates — this was the cause you should have championed. You talked about empowerment, but never looked at where women are truly disempowered: in the home, after childbirth, when society shrugs and walks away.

If you won't fight for mothers, someone else will. Because without mothers, there is no future.

And without a future, your ideology — no matter how sophisticated or progressive — means absolutely nothing.

The Feminism That Forgot the Majority

Feminism loves to celebrate its wins in the boardroom. You hear the stories everywhere: women breaking glass ceilings, securing corner offices, dominating industries once reserved for men. These victories get headlines, book deals, and keynote speeches. But while feminism champions these high-profile battles, it conveniently turns a blind eye to the millions of women who are nowhere near those glass ceilings — the ones who keep the world turning with their sweat, muscle, and relentless grind.

The problem is clear: feminism's definition of "women in the workforce" is narrow, elitist, and exclusionary. It means women in suits, with degrees, who play corporate politics and network at power lunches. The rest—the factory workers, janitors, cashiers, house cleaners, and single mothers juggling multiple jobs—are left out in the cold. Their labour is invisible, their struggles ignored, and their needs dismissed.

If you aren't an Ivy League intern, a marketing executive, or a Silicon Valley coder, feminism doesn't care about you. You don't make the agenda. Your workplace injuries, your lack of paid maternity leave, your fight for affordable childcare, your zero sick days, your minimum wage — none of it registers on the feminist radar.

It's not just an oversight; it's a systematic erasure. Feminism's obsession with a particular type of "professional woman" has created a hierarchy of struggle, where the ambitions of a few elite women count far more than the daily hardships faced by the majority.

Consider this: the very jobs feminism ignores are the ones that keep society functioning. Without factory workers, there are no goods to sell. Without cleaners, offices and hospitals become unlivable. Without cashiers, retail grinds to a halt. Without caregivers, often unrecognized and unpaid, our children and the elderly suffer. Yet feminism focuses on "breaking the glass ceiling," not "breaking the glass walls" that cage millions of working-class women in low pay, precarious conditions, and no benefits.

Even more glaring is how feminism treats caregiving and homemaking. The vast majority of unpaid labour in homes—childcare, eldercare, cooking, cleaning—is done by women, yet it's treated like a personal hobby rather than essential economic work. Feminism, with its obsession with career and salary, dismisses these roles as "regressive" or "settling," effectively shaming women who prioritize family or cannot enter the "professional" workforce.

And when it comes to benefits and protections—things like paid maternity leave, sick days, flexible hours—the disparity between women in elite positions and those in low-wage hourly jobs couldn't be starker. Executives enjoy generous family leave policies, private childcare, and flexible schedules, while millions of working-class women have none of these. In fact, for many hourly workers, missing a day means losing pay, or worse, losing their job entirely. Yet feminism has done little to challenge this reality.

Why? Because these women don't fit the narrative. They don't wear business suits or speak at conferences. Their struggles don't sell books or attract media attention. The feminist movement has been hijacked by a privileged minority that prioritizes its gains over the collective good.

This isn't just a critique — it's a call to action. If feminism truly claims to represent *all* women, it must shed this narrow, elitist focus and expand its fight to include the invisible majority. It must advocate for paid sick leave for cleaners, hazard pay for factory workers, affordable childcare for single mothers, and the recognition that caregiving is work, not a personal sacrifice.

Until then, feminism is a movement divided, serving the interests of a few at the expense of the many. Its victories may shine in boardrooms, but they are hollow victories — because outside those offices, millions of women remain invisible, vulnerable, and ignored.

And without those women, without their labour, without their sacrifices, there is no boardroom to break into.

The Invisible Majority: Homemakers, Hourly Workers, Caregivers

Who's out there fighting for the cleaners who spend their days scrubbing floors and toilets? Who's raising their voice for the cashiers standing for hours on end, with no breaks, under fluorescent lights? What about the factory workers who face constant physical strain, repetitive injuries, and dangerous machinery? Or the hospital janitors who keep our health facilities clean and safe but have zero job security, no paid sick leave, and certainly no maternity benefits?

The truth is, there isn't a feminist movement for these women — the backbone of every economy and every community — because feminism has chosen to ignore them. These women don't make headlines, don't get invited to glossy conferences, and don't have the luxury of time to network or campaign for their rights. They punch clocks, work overtime, and face workplace hazards without applause or recognition.

Feminism has prioritized a certain image of "empowerment" — the polished executive, the Ivy League graduate, the startup CEO — while leaving out the millions of women whose work is essential but unglamorous. These women's jobs aren't "empowering" in the feminist playbook because they don't come with corner offices, stock options, or fancy job titles. Instead, they come with low wages, zero benefits, unpredictable schedules, and relentless physical demands.

And what about homemakers? The millions of women who manage households, raise children, care for elderly relatives, and keep the wheels turning without pay? Feminism treats homemaking as a fallback or a concession — a "choice" that somehow diminishes a woman's worth. The unpaid labour of homemakers is dismissed as "not real work," erased from economic calculations and feminist policy debates.

This is a damning failure. Because without these invisible workers and caregivers, the economy collapses. Without them, the so-called empowered women in boardrooms would have no offices to run, no children to educate, no homes to return to.

It's time to call out feminism for what it is: a movement that has lost touch with the majority of women. The ones who don't just want a seat at the corporate table — they want dignity, fairness, and protections for the work they already do. Until feminism embraces these women, it's not fighting for *all* women — only a privileged few.

The invisible majority demands recognition. Not charity, not tokenism, but real policies that address their daily struggles. Paid sick leave, fair wages, affordable childcare, protections from workplace abuse, and respect for caregiving as essential labour.

Because when the invisible majority rises, feminism will either evolve or become irrelevant.

The Myth of Universal Feminism

Feminism loves to shout about "choice" — but whose choice are we really talking about? It's the choice of a privileged few: the women with access to elite education, cushy office jobs, and flexible schedules. The ones who can afford to take expensive childcare or outsource household work. The women who climb corporate ladders, break glass ceilings, and rack up LinkedIn endorsements.

But what about the millions of women who don't get to pick from a buffet of career and lifestyle options? The women who *have* to stay home because childcare costs more than their paycheck. The women who juggle multiple jobs, or work hourly gigs with no benefits and zero job security, just to keep their families afloat. Feminism doesn't seem to have a place for them.

In feminist rhetoric, a woman who leaves the workforce to care for her children is often dismissed as a "dropout," a "failure," or someone who "gave up." No marches. No speeches. No hashtags. Just silent judgment. Because in the feminist narrative, motherhood is treated as a footnote — a regressive choice, a sacrifice women supposedly make *against* progress.

This hypocrisy cuts deep. Feminism claims to fight for *all* women, but it fails to acknowledge the most fundamental role many women play: raising the next generation. Instead of support and celebration, mothers face stigma and economic penalties. They get no awards at conferences, no policy wins, no real respect.

And make no mistake — this isn't accidental. It's a deliberate blindness to the realities that don't fit the preferred feminist storyline. Motherhood, caregiving, homemaking — these are powerful acts that sustain society, yet feminism sidelines them as backward or irrelevant.

If feminism truly cared about choice, it would recognize that choosing to be a mother, or needing to be one, is just as valid as choosing to be a CEO. It would fight for policies that make motherhood viable without economic punishment — paid parental leave, affordable childcare, workplace flexibility, and, yes, meaningful tax breaks.

Until then, feminism is a myth of universality — an elite club that applauds a narrow slice of women while ignoring the rest. The women who build families, keep homes, and hold communities together remain invisible in its agenda.

No Benefits for the Working-Class Woman

Let's get real: the vast majority of women won't be CEOs, managers, or power players in glass towers. Most women clock in and out of jobs that pay by the hour — retail, cleaning, factory floors, caregiving, hospitality. Jobs where "paid maternity leave" and "flexible hours" are pipe dreams. Missing one day means losing a paycheck. Taking time off for childbirth or sick kids? Forget it.

And where is feminism in all this? Nowhere to be found. While the movement champions corner offices and corporate perks, it has turned a blind eye to the working-class women who keep the economy alive. These women bear the heaviest burdens — physically demanding work, job insecurity, and no safety net — yet they get no feminist rallying cries, no policy wins, no national spotlight.

This isn't just negligence; it's a betrayal. Feminism has built its brand on equality, but fails to tackle the glaring inequalities that hurt millions of everyday women. Women who can't afford nannies, who face wage theft, who live paycheck to paycheck, and who have zero access to basic benefits that many take for granted.

Paid sick leave? Maternity leave? Affordable childcare? Workplace protections? These are *life-or-death* issues for working-class women. Yet feminism's agenda rarely includes them. Instead, it remains obsessed with the shiny few who wear suits and heels, ignoring that these benefits matter far more to the woman on the assembly line or behind the cash register.

The cold truth: the working-class woman's struggle is feminism's greatest failure. Until feminism fights for *her*, it's not fighting for all women. It's time to stop celebrating privilege and start championing the needs of the invisible majority.

Feminism's Class Blindness is a Moral Failure

Feminism preaches equality, but only for a narrow slice of women. The shiny image of female empowerment is built on the backs of millions of working-class women who remain invisible, underpaid, and utterly unsupported. It's no accident that feminism sidelines the vast majority; it's a conscious, systemic choice.

This class blindness isn't just a flaw—it's a moral failure. By ignoring the realities of women who don't fit the privileged mould, feminism fractures its base and betrays its foundational promise of equality. It divides women into "worthy" and "unworthy," creating a hierarchy where status and income determine who gets a voice and who stays silent.

Meanwhile, millions of women—homemakers, factory workers, cashiers, caregivers—are left to struggle alone, with no union, no advocacy, and no policy to protect them. They're not just overlooked; they're erased.

If feminism truly claims to fight for *all* women, it must confront this divide head-on. It means dismantling elitism within the movement and redirecting energy towards the struggles that affect the majority. Until then, feminism will remain a club for the privileged few, leaving countless women behind and weakening the cause of real equality.

Why Feminism's Class Blindness Is a Recipe for Failure

Feminism has long claimed to be the champion of all women's rights, promising equality, empowerment, and liberation. Yet, the reality reveals a glaring contradiction: the movement has consistently prioritized the interests of a narrow, privileged class while leaving millions of working-class women invisible and voiceless. This class blindness is not a mere oversight or accidental side effect—it carries profound implications that threaten not only the legitimacy and effectiveness of feminism but also the broader social and economic well-being of women everywhere.

1. Deepening Social Divisions Among Women

When feminism elevates the concerns of upper-middle-class professionals and sidelines the struggles of hourly workers, caregivers, and homemakers, it fractures the very community it claims to unite. Instead of solidarity, it breeds resentment and alienation. Working-class women see feminism as an exclusive club of boardroom women and Ivy League grads, disconnected from their realities. This division undermines collective action, weakens political power, and stalls progress on issues that affect all women, such as fair wages, affordable childcare, healthcare access, and workplace protections.

Rather than building bridges, feminism's class blindness erects walls. The result is a fractured movement where the priorities of the privileged drown out the urgent needs of the majority.

2. The Erosion of Feminism's Moral Authority

Feminism's credibility depends on its claim to represent *all* women. When it ignores large swaths of the female population struggling with job insecurity, lack of paid leave, unpredictable schedules, and poverty, it loses its moral high ground. Critics are quick to point out this hypocrisy, and rightfully so.

This erosion of moral authority invites backlash from both women and men who feel feminism no longer speaks for them. It fuels narratives that feminism is elitist, out of touch, and irrelevant. Worse, it opens the door for reactionary forces to co-opt women's issues with superficial lip service, offering token gestures that do little to address real systemic problems.

3. Policy Neglect and Economic Vulnerability

Because feminism focuses primarily on professional women's concerns, like breaking glass ceilings or achieving corporate quotas, policy advocacy often neglects the most pressing needs of working-class women. Issues such as paid sick leave, fair scheduling laws, affordable childcare, workplace safety, and living wages are frequently sidelined in favour of debates about CEO representation or gender diversity initiatives in tech firms.

THE GREAT FEMINISM SCAM

This policy neglect leaves millions of women economically vulnerable. Without support, many working-class women face impossible choices: miss work and lose income, or risk their health and well-being by showing up sick or exhausted. The absence of a feminist voice championing these issues perpetuates cycles of poverty and limits women's true economic independence.

4. Reinforcing Patriarchy Through Class

Feminism's focus on elite careers often inadvertently reinforces patriarchal norms. By defining success narrowly as corporate achievement, it upholds capitalist and patriarchal structures that value productivity and profit over caregiving and community. This leaves women who choose or need to work in caregiving roles, domestic labour, or less prestigious jobs marginalized and undervalued.

Ironically, this narrow definition of empowerment denies women the full range of choices feminism claims to support. It punishes motherhood and caregiving by ignoring their economic and social value, further entrenching gender inequalities in both public and private spheres.

5. Missed Opportunities for Broader Social Change

Had feminism embraced working-class women's struggles as central rather than peripheral, the movement could have harnessed a much larger, more diverse coalition. This broader base could push for systemic reforms that benefit all women—better labour laws, universal childcare, stronger social safety nets, and equitable healthcare.

By focusing mostly on elite women, feminism has missed an opportunity to transform the economic and social structures that oppress *all* women. Instead, it risks becoming a narrowly focused interest group, constrained by the limits of its own class biases.

The Path Forward: What Feminism Must Do

For feminism to reclaim its promise of true equality, it must confront the glaring class blindness that has fractured its ranks and limited its impact. This is not about merely adding working-class women to the conversation as an afterthought. It is about fundamentally reshaping the movement's priorities, language, and policies so that they reflect the realities of the majority of women—those who clean offices, care for children without paid leave, work factory shifts, and manage households on tight budgets.

Centring the Voices and Experiences of Working-Class Women

A movement that claims to fight for *all* women cannot afford to silence or marginalize the voices of those who do the hardest, most undervalued labour. Feminism must actively listen to and elevate the stories of women whose work goes unseen, whether that work is in a factory, on the cleaning crew, or raising children at home. These experiences aren't just anecdotes; they reveal systemic failures and barriers that the current feminist agenda often ignores.

True inclusion means reshaping feminist spaces, from conferences to policy discussions, so that working-class women and caregivers have real power and representation, not token seats. It means prioritizing their concerns as foundational, not peripheral.

Advocating for Economic Security, Labour Rights, and Social Supports for Hourly Workers

Economic justice for women must move beyond the glass ceiling obsession to address the glass floor beneath millions of workers who lack basic protections. Feminism must champion paid sick leave, maternity and parental leave for hourly workers, fair scheduling laws, living wages, affordable childcare, and healthcare access.

These issues aren't "women's issues" in isolation—they are economic and human rights issues. By fighting for these policies, feminism can become a driving force for broad-based social justice that uplifts entire communities, not just privileged individuals.

Revaluing Caregiving and Domestic Labour as Essential and Worthy of Economic Recognition

Motherhood and caregiving have long been treated as invisible duties, unworthy of fair compensation or respect. Feminism must challenge this devaluation by insisting that caregiving labour is essential work that sustains society and deserves economic recognition, whether through paid family leave, caregiving stipends, or social security credits.

This requires a radical shift away from capitalist valuations that prioritize profit over people and recognize that the future of any nation depends on the well-being of those who nurture and raise the next generation.

Building Solidarity Across Class Lines to Strengthen Collective Power

Class divisions weaken women's collective power. Feminism must reject elitism and build genuine solidarity between professional women and working-class women. This means organizing across workplaces, unions, and communities to demand rights and respect for all.

Collective bargaining and grassroots activism must become core strategies in the feminist toolkit, reconnecting the movement to labour struggles and economic justice campaigns that have historically lifted working-class women.

Rejecting Elitism and Embracing an Inclusive Vision of Empowerment

Empowerment is not one-size-fits-all. Feminism must abandon the narrow idea that empowerment equals climbing the corporate ladder or holding high-status jobs. True empowerment respects diverse choices and circumstances—whether that means pursuing a professional career, raising a family, or balancing both under difficult conditions.

By embracing an inclusive vision, feminism can dismantle judgment and division among women and instead foster mutual respect and support.

Feminism's future depends on its ability to confront uncomfortable truths about class and privilege within its ranks. Ignoring the struggles of working-class women and caregivers is no longer an option if the movement wants to remain relevant and just.

The feminism of tomorrow must be intersectional, not only in theory but in practice—class-conscious, inclusive, and boldly committed to economic justice for all women. Only then can it fulfill its original promise: to dismantle all forms of oppression and build a society where every woman, regardless of her job or background, can live with dignity, security, and true equality.

Anything less risks leaving millions behind—and with them, the future of feminism itself.

Feminism's Most Convenient Lies

Abortion as Freedom: How Choice Turned into Silent Pressure

The Silence Around Regret: A Feminist Blind Spot

For a movement that claims to uplift all women, mainstream feminism has cultivated a surprising intolerance for emotional nuance around abortion. The narrative is often binary: abortion equals empowerment, while carrying an unplanned pregnancy equates to submission. But what about the women who don't feel empowered? What about those who feel sadness, ambivalence, or regret?

These women are often shunned, or worse, erased. Their voices don't fit the curated image of the strong, independent woman who "chose" her freedom. In reality, many women don't feel they have a choice at all—they feel cornered. When access to healthcare, childcare, housing, and meaningful male partnership is lacking, the "freedom to choose" quickly becomes a choice between two losses: sacrifice your body and future or sacrifice a life you're not prepared to support.

Cultural Pressures Disguised as Liberation

Modern feminism claims to fight patriarchy, yet it often reinforces a system that treats female fertility as a liability. Women are subtly (and not-so-subtly) told that pregnancy will ruin their careers, figures, and freedom. In this climate, abortion isn't just an option—it becomes the expected response to unplanned pregnancy. Saying "no" to abortion requires a woman to defy the prevailing cultural winds and risk being judged as irresponsible, regressive, or naive.

The pressure isn't always overt. It's in the boyfriend who says he "supports whatever you decide," while making it clear that fatherhood is off the table. It's in the female friends who imply that keeping the baby means wasting your life. It's in the quiet implication that a strong, empowered woman doesn't get "stuck" with a child.

Who Really Benefits?

This version of abortion freedom serves others more than it serves women. It lets men off the hook. It absolves society of the need to build structures that support mothers. It keeps women in the workforce without disrupting the flow of productivity or demanding workplace reform. And it allows feminism to claim a symbolic win, even if it leaves many women feeling hollow, alone, and unheard.

When women are told that their pain, regret, or longing for motherhood is invalid—or worse, a betrayal of the cause—they're not being empowered. They're being used. Real empowerment would mean supporting all women's choices—including those who choose motherhood under less-than-ideal circumstances—and building a world where abortion isn't a silent obligation, but a last resort.

The Rise of Sex Positivity and the Exploitation of Desire

When Empowerment Becomes Obligation

What began as a rebellion against puritanical sexual shame has, paradoxically, created a new kind of pressure: performative liberation. Under the banner of sex positivity, many women feel compelled to say "yes" not because they truly want to, but because saying "no" would be seen as prudish, repressed, or "not evolved." Feminism, in its modern form, now too often rewards conformity to a hypersexual script—ironically, the same script patriarchy once imposed.

This has transformed consent into choreography. Sex becomes something to perform rather than something to experience with agency and intention. And when women push back, questioning the emotional toll of hookup culture or the pressure to be endlessly available, they are accused of internalized misogyny rather than being listened to.

A Marketplace of the Body

The commercialization of sex positivity has only accelerated the exploitation. From "sex work is work" slogans to the glamorization of platforms like OnlyFans, women are told that selling their bodies is not only acceptable but empowering. Yet the reality often involves economic coercion, blurred boundaries, and mental health fallout. The line between liberation and commodification grows ever thinner.

Corporations and online platforms profit from this cultural shift, marketing hypersexuality as self-expression while conveniently ignoring the physical and psychological risks. It's liberation for sale—but the cost is rarely discussed.

Reclaiming Real Agency

True sexual agency is not about how much sex you have—it's about having the power to choose, free of pressure, judgment, or ideological coercion. That includes the power to say *no*, value emotional intimacy, set boundaries, or abstain entirely. But this version of agency isn't marketable. It doesn't drive

79

clicks, subscriptions, or ad revenue. So it's drowned out by louder voices insisting that liberation looks like exhibitionism, that pleasure is proof of power, and that questioning the narrative makes you a traitor to the cause.

Sex positivity, in its current form, often demands that women conform to a new norm while pretending they're freer than ever. The truth is, desire is not empowerment unless it's truly your own.

The OnlyFans Trap: Branding Self-Exploitation as Empowerment

The Commodification of Consent

The allure of OnlyFans lies in its promise of autonomy—control over content, pricing, and engagement. But this so-called control often exists within rigid, invisible boundaries set by demand. What sells is not what empowers, but what pleases. And so the myth of agency becomes a performance tailored to male consumption.

Women are told that they are reclaiming their bodies by selling access to them, but the transaction still mimics old dynamics: men as buyers, women as objects. The difference now is that the packaging is done by feminism. It's branded as liberation, but the labour remains deeply gendered and often exploitative.

When the Hustle Becomes a Cage

Even for the minority of creators who earn well, the pressure to maintain engagement can become all-consuming. Every post, every message, every photo becomes part of a relentless marketing strategy—one that demands constant sexual availability and emotional labour. This is not freedom; it is an endless hustle performed under the gaze of paying strangers.

And for the majority who earn little or nothing, the risks vastly outweigh the rewards: loss of privacy, future employability, family estrangement, and growing mental health struggles. But these stories rarely make it into feminist discussions, because they complicate the tidy narrative of choice and empowerment.

A System Dressed in Liberation

What modern feminism often refuses to admit is that many women turn to platforms like OnlyFans not out of empowerment but out of necessity. Rent is due. Debt is crushing. Job options are limited. In this context, "choice" becomes a hollow word.

This is not sexual liberation—it is economic survival wrapped in seductive hashtags. And yet, critique is often met with hostility, as if acknowledging the exploitative aspects of sex work is somehow anti-woman. But real feminism should be strong enough to face uncomfortable truths, not paper over them with slogans.

Until then, OnlyFans remains not a platform of empowerment, but a mirror reflecting how deeply capitalism and patriarchy have learned to wear feminism's face.

Pornified Feminism: Surviving on Patriarchy's Terms

Empowerment or Compliance?

Pornified feminism offers a seductive lie: that participation in self-sexualization equals control. But control over the terms of your objectification is not the same as liberation from it. When the dominant path to cultural relevance, financial gain, or even social capital for women is through hypersexual visibility, that is not freedom—it is adaptation.

What's framed as feminist expression often mirrors the same scripts long written by the male gaze. TikTok dances, Instagram thirst traps, and fashion trends inspired by pornographic aesthetics are not subversive simply because women post them willingly. Consent doesn't erase context.

The Burden of Constant Visibility

Modern womanhood, under the pornified gaze, demands perpetual performance. Be sexy, but not too sexy. Be confident, but not threatening. Be available, but pretend it's all on your terms. The cost of not participating in this game? Invisibility. Irrelevance. Judgment.

Feminism once fought for a world where women could be valued beyond their bodies. Today, that fight is often drowned out by applause for those who play the part well. The pressure to conform to hypersexual norms isn't liberation—it's labour. And it's labour that disproportionately affects young girls who learn early that their worth is often tied to their desirability.

The Illusion of Subversion

Pornified feminism insists that reclaiming slut or bimbo identities is a subversive act. But what does it say about the feminist movement when power is found not in resisting the male gaze, but in performing for it? Subversion requires disruption, not repetition with new branding.

If empowerment always looks like lingerie photos, strip teases, or public sexual displays, then we must ask: who benefits? Who is watching? And who would still care if women stopped performing?

True liberation lies in expanding the definitions of power, not reinforcing the narrowest, most marketable ones.

Corporate Feminism and the 'Girlboss' Illusion

Success on Whose Terms?

The "girlboss" archetype promised women that they could have it all—career, influence, independence—if they just worked hard enough. But what it delivered was a rebranded version of male ambition in stilettos. Instead of dismantling the structures that marginalized women, it taught them how to mimic the behaviours that built those structures in the first place.

Workplaces were never redesigned for balance, collaboration, or care. Instead, women were encouraged to perform competitiveness, stoicism, and overwork, not as survival tactics, but as empowerment. The reward? Stress, anxiety, and the illusion of progress.

Feminism for Sale

Corporate feminism thrives by reducing liberation to lifestyle. You're not underpaid—you just need to negotiate better. You're not burned out—you need a better planner, a matcha latte, and a gratitude journal. The system remains untouched, but you're told you're failing at self-care.

Brands capitalize on this by selling empowerment as a product. Every lipstick, tote bag, and yoga app becomes a tool of self-actualization. The market doesn't just co-opt feminism—it turns it into a revenue stream. Power is redefined not by collective transformation, but by purchasing power and personal hustle.

The Myth of Having It All

The "have it all" mantra has become a cruel joke. Behind every polished LinkedIn post is a woman juggling impossible expectations: performative success at work, emotional labour at home, and curated perfection online. When these women falter—as anyone would under such conditions—they're told to fix themselves, not the system.

The girlboss movement pretended to break glass ceilings but left the floor untouched. Women made it into boardrooms, but many found themselves more isolated than ever—tokenized, overextended, and still expected to smile.

From Individualism to Solidarity

Real feminism should not be about putting more women into oppressive systems. It should be about transforming those systems altogether. The goal is not to make women better cogs—it's to question the machine.

Until the conversation shifts from personal branding to structural change, the girlboss remains a hollow symbol: powerful in image, powerless in impact.

How We Got Here: From Social Contracts to Swipe Culture

From Courtship to Consumption

Traditional courtship, though far from perfect, demanded effort. It asked men to show consistency, seriousness, and sacrifice before gaining intimacy. This wasn't just romantic idealism; it created social friction that helped filter out unserious intentions. The norms incentivized men to rise to the occasion and provided women with a kind of cultural leverage.

In contrast, dating apps have collapsed this entire process into a game of low-stakes browsing. Relationships are no longer built—they're skimmed, selected, and discarded like products. Swiping culture turns people into options rather than partners, reducing intimacy to instant gratification. For women, this has meant being constantly accessible, yet increasingly undervalued.

Sexual Freedom or Sexual Bargaining?

Second-wave feminism sought to decouple sex from obligation. But in removing sex from emotional context and commitment, it unintentionally removed the guardrails. What was meant to liberate women from shame also removed societal expectations on men. Now, many women find themselves stuck in a loop of meaningless encounters, hoping emotional connection might eventually follow physical intimacy.

Instead of giving women more power, the new script often leaves them with less. They give more, emotionally and physically, while receiving less: less commitment, less clarity, and less care.

The Disappearing Man

Where past generations attached consequences to male withdrawal (both social and financial), the current landscape enables easy exits. Ghosting, breadcrumbing, and non-committal "situationships" have become normalized. The expectation that a man should take responsibility for a woman he sleeps with is now seen as outdated, even oppressive.

But the consequences haven't disappeared—they've simply shifted. Women are now expected to absorb the fallout of hookup culture: navigating heartbreak, abortion, solo parenting, or lifelong sexual health implications, all under the banner of choice.

Choice Without Structure Is Not Freedom

Feminism promised women freedom of choice, but did not ensure that those choices came with societal support or male accountability. In the name of dismantling patriarchy, it dismantled the few structures that asked something of men in return.

In their place is a deregulated market of desire where the highest bidder is usually the one who offers the least: least effort, least vulnerability, and least responsibility. Women are told they can have it all, but they're left holding all the risk.

The Illusion of Sexual Freedom

Freedom or Just a New Double Standard?

Sexual freedom was sold as a form of emancipation, liberating women from the shame and stigma that had long policed their bodies. But in practice, that "freedom" has been asymmetrical. It unshackled men from responsibility while burdening women with the full spectrum of risks and consequences.

In this framework, a woman's availability becomes expected, not celebrated. Meanwhile, her emotional needs are often dismissed as clingy, naïve, or retrograde. What was once seen as intimacy is now just a transaction, and what was once protection is now portrayed as oppression.

The Disappearing Cost for Men

Technological advances like birth control and legal abortion have certainly given women more control over reproduction. But paradoxically, they've also enabled men to disengage even further. When a man hears that a woman is on the pill or supports abortion rights, many interpret this not as empowerment, but as a green light to act without thought or consequence.

He doesn't need to worry about children. He doesn't need to worry about commitment. And if pregnancy happens? That's "her choice," and by extension, her problem.

The Loneliness of Consequence

The physical toll—side effects from hormonal contraceptives, invasive procedures, the trauma of abortion—is often shouldered in silence. The emotional toll—regret, shame, lost self-worth—gets buried beneath a mountain of slogans: *My body, my choice, Shout your abortion, Sex is power.*

But for the woman left crying alone in a clinic, or the one quietly wondering if that one night cost her her fertility, these slogans offer little comfort. Feminism, in its mainstream form, often fails to meet these women where they are, choosing instead to erase their grief for fear it will be weaponized by conservatives.

When Empowerment Becomes Gaslighting

To express pain or regret in this landscape is to risk being seen as weak—or worse, a traitor to the cause. Women are taught to deny their discomfort or rationalize it as "part of the journey." And if they can't do that, they're subtly told they must be the exception, the one who "didn't do it right."

True empowerment should make space for contradiction. It should allow a woman to say: *I wanted freedom, but this hurt me.* Instead, modern discourse often gaslights women into silence, pressuring them to wear their trauma like a badge of honour, or to pretend it doesn't exist at all.

The Price of the Lie

Modern feminism has spun a seductive narrative: that liberation lies in sex without consequence, careers without limits, and choices beyond judgment. But in reality, these promises have merely replaced old constraints with new ones—quieter, internal, and harder to name.

Women are told that freedom means behaving like men, but never warned that the systems they're entering were never built to nurture anyone. They are asked to give more of themselves—to jobs, to lovers, to platforms that profit off their bodies—and to call it empowerment.

But when empowerment feels like burnout, and when freedom looks like fallout, it's time to ask: has the movement lost its way?

Feminism must stop selling half-truths dressed as progress. It must stop confusing commodification with choice, and pain with strength. If it truly seeks liberation, it must start by telling the whole story—even the parts that can't be hashtagged.

Only then can it reclaim its purpose—and become a movement worth believing in again.

The Child Marriage Hypocrisy

Legal at 16 — As Long As It's Marriage

Let's talk legal logic—Canada edition. At 16, you can't buy alcohol. You can't vote for the people making your laws. You can't rent a car or a hotel room. You can't even sign a cell phone contract without a guardian. But somehow, you *can* sign a marriage certificate and legally become someone's spouse. That's right: you're not mature enough to toast your own wedding, but you're apparently mature enough to be in one.

Now, before someone chimes in with "parental consent is required," let's think about that for a second. If you *need* your parents' permission, doesn't that inherently mean you're not a fully autonomous adult yet? So why, then, are we letting non-adults enter what is arguably the most legally binding, emotionally taxing, and financially entangling institution we have? If 16-year-olds aren't trusted to decide whether to get a tattoo without their parents' blessing, why are we letting them decide—or worse, be *pushed into*—marriage?

This isn't some forgotten relic of a long-dead era. These laws are *active*. They are functioning in real-time. And no, they're not only found in some hyper-religious backwoods community with 12-person school boards and a single shared family tractor. Canada, one of the most "progressive" countries in the world, still allows this. Only Manitoba has drawn a clear line in the sand by setting the minimum marriage age at 18 without exception. The rest? They've apparently decided that if you're old enough to cram for biology exams, you're old enough to start a family.

And let's be honest, "parental consent" is often a polite euphemism for "paternal permission." Because in most cases, it's not the young bride storming into the courthouse with stars in her eyes—it's a much older man convincing her parents that he's a stand-up guy and would make a "good husband." Translation: "I'll take her off your hands. Think of the financial savings."

Of course, we love to talk about *choice*. But when that choice comes attached to a father's nod of approval and a culture that still views girls as liabilities with expiration dates, let's not pretend this is all sunshine and empowerment.

And here's the punchline no one asked for: that same girl, freshly married at 16, couldn't go on a honeymoon to Las Vegas because she's not old enough to check into a hotel room on her own. But she's old enough to sign up for a lifetime of emotional labour, potential

THE GREAT FEMINISM SCAM

pregnancies, and a possible divorce settlement before she can legally rent a Zipcar.

Canada: where childhood ends at "I do."

Falling in Love... with a 50-Year-Old?

We all grew up on stories of young love—Romeo and Juliet sneaking around balconies, declaring eternal devotion before they've even figured out what taxes are. But Canada's version of this modern fairytale? Picture Juliet as a 10th grader and Romeo as someone who needs Viagra and qualifies for a pension.

Yes, these laws are marketed as safeguards for "young couples in love" who just can't wait to spend forever together. But let's be honest—how often is the groom also worrying about finishing high school? The reality isn't high school sweethearts running to city hall. It's middle-aged men, sometimes older than the girl's father, smoothing things over with mom and dad so they can legally wed someone who just started using deodorant regularly.

Let's spell it out: this isn't love. This isn't romance. This is grooming with legal stationery. A 50-year-old man doesn't "fall in love" with a teenager because of shared life experience or riveting intellectual chemistry. He falls in love with power dynamics—specifically, the kind that ensure he always has the upper hand. She's not his partner; she's his project.

And yet, as long as she's 16 and he's got a charming enough smile (or wallet), he can make her his wife. Legally. No police. No protests. No public outcry. Just a cake, some signatures, and an entire adult life redirected.

We have harsher age restrictions on TikTok features than we do on marriage laws. Let that sink in.

And feminists? Nowhere to be found. Because, apparently, protecting a 16-year-old girl from becoming the third wife of a guy old enough to have witnessed the birth of the internet isn't as trendy as fighting for the CEO pay gap between two Ivy League grads.

Let's quit pretending this is about love. It's not. It's abuse, with better lighting and a guest list.

The Sex Part: Even Easier

Now here's the plot twist nobody asked for: while marriage at 16 still needs a parental permission slip, sex does not. That's right—Canada's age of sexual consent is 16. No note from mom required. No wedding bells needed. Just a birthday, and boom: it's legally open season.

Translation? A 55-year-old man can sleep with a teenager who still asks permission to go to the bathroom, and the law will shrug. Why? Because she said yes, despite the fact that she probably can't yet say "no" to a pushy prom date without doubting herself for days.

We're supposed to believe that a girl who needs a signed form to go on a field trip is suddenly equipped to make life-altering decisions about sex with someone four decades her senior. Sure. That makes sense. Right up there with putting a toddler behind the wheel because they've "seen you drive enough times."

This isn't about protecting youth. It's about providing legal cover for creeps. And let's be honest: the guy with a mortgage, a receding hairline, and a granddaughter in the same math class? He's not interested in "mutual consent." He's interested in control—emotional, psychological, and legal.

And somehow, feminists have stayed silent on this, too. The same movement that will march over a rude joke on Twitter suddenly goes mute when it comes to age-gap exploitation that's basically gift-wrapped in law. Why? Because talking about this would mean addressing the uncomfortable truth that not all "consensual" relationships are harmless, and not all abuse leaves bruises.

Let's be real: this isn't consent. It's a loophole. A giant, gaping one that predators can sprint through with impunity, waving their legal get-out-of-jail-free card.

Because once she turns 16, society stops asking whether she understands what she's saying yes to. It only asks whether she said it.

Three Marriages Before She Can Drink

Imagine this timeline: A girl gets married at 16 with her parents' blessing (read: pressure). She's pregnant at 17. Divorced before she figures out how to file taxes. By 17 and a half, she's back in a wedding dress. Divorced again before grad photos. At 18, she walks down the aisle for a third time—still too young to legally toast with champagne at her own reception.

Meanwhile, you need to be 19 to buy alcohol in most provinces. Because apparently choosing a lifelong partner, raising a child, and navigating custody battles is fine, but choosing a drink? That's too much responsibility.

These contradictions aren't just laughable—they're dangerous. They reveal a legal system more comfortable with teen girls entering marriages than entering nightclubs. More ready to rubber-stamp a wedding license than a student loan. More concerned with protecting "tradition" than protecting minors.

And yet, this circus of contradictions rolls on—uninterrupted, unchallenged, and largely unmentioned by the very people who claim to fight for women's rights.

Because God forbid we upset the status quo by asking why a girl can have two kids before her first legal White Claw.

Where Is Feminism?

Now comes the part no one likes to say out loud: feminism isn't showing up for these girls.

You'd think a movement built on smashing the patriarchy would throw everything it's got at the idea of teenage girls being legally married off to men three times their age. You'd expect marches. Op-eds. Hashtags. Maybe even a podcast or two.

But no.

Not a whisper. Not a movement. Not even a strongly worded tweet.

Why? Because this issue isn't sexy. It doesn't come with influencer-friendly optics or viral potential. No one's handing out brand deals for protecting poor, rural 16-year-olds from marriage proposals that sound more like retirement home power plays than love stories.

There's no girlbossing your way out of this kind of exploitation. No glossy campaign about a Grade 10 student being convinced to marry someone old enough to be her grandfather. No TED Talk about the trauma of being divorced with two kids before your first vote.

So the cause is left in the dust. Too messy. Too inconvenient. Too real.

Because modern feminism, for all its slogans about "choice" and "liberation," still chooses its battles based on aesthetics, not urgency.

And protecting girls who haven't made it to university—or even their prom—just doesn't fit the vibe.

The Selective Activism Problem

Modern feminism has a type. And it's not shy about it.

She's got a degree, probably from an Ivy League school. She drinks overpriced coffee. She talks about glass ceilings on LinkedIn. She has a skincare routine *and* a publicist. And feminism shows up for her every time, with articles, panels, and hashtags that sparkle with empowerment.

But the 16-year-old girl being quietly married off by her parents to a 50-year-old man? Crickets.

No trendy graphics. No solidarity posts. No candlelight vigils. Just silence and the sound of a government form being signed.

Because this kind of activism likes microphones, not uncomfortable truths. It's easier to fight for boardroom equity than to step into a trailer park and ask why a teenager is in a wedding dress instead of a school uniform.

And that's the real problem: feminism keeps forgetting the women who don't have a platform, a PR team, or a seat at the brunch table.

If your feminism only shows up when there are cameras, then maybe it's not about justice—it's just branding.

Because if it can't protect the most vulnerable girls—the ones who are still being legally handed over like property—then we have to ask the uncomfortable question:

Who is feminism really for?

Majority Rules, But Nothing Changes

Let's talk numbers. Women make up more than half the population. They outvote men in most democratic elections. Statistically, women have the political power to shape entire countries. If every woman in Canada decided tomorrow that child marriage was unacceptable, the laws could be changed within a single legislative cycle. Done. Over. Gone.

And yet—here we are.

The law still allows a 16-year-old to marry a man old enough to have babysat her mother. Still allows parents to hand over their daughters like they're trading goats in a dowry deal. Still pretends that "parental consent" is some magical safeguard, even when it's often the very thing being abused.

How is this still a thing?

Despite having the numbers, the votes, and the moral high ground, nothing changes. Why? Because the outrage is selective. It's easier to rally behind glass ceilings and boardroom diversity than to get messy with something as uncomfortable as child marriage. It's easier to push for equal pay at Fortune 500 companies than to stop a 60-year-old man from legally marrying a 10th grader in Ontario.

Legislators don't act. Activists stay quiet. The media yawns. And the cycle goes on.

Let's be clear: this isn't about political apathy. It's about political convenience. It's about which issues are fashionable, photogenic, and easy to package into digestible campaigns. And this one—this grim, awkward, deeply unsettling reality—just isn't it.

But here's the punchline: if a woman can organize a national protest over a tampon tax, surely she can spare five minutes to call her MP and say, "Hey, maybe let's not legalize child brides."

And if she doesn't?

Well, then we have to ask the uncomfortable question: With the majority of votes, the majority of consumer power, and the majority of representation in many advocacy spaces, if women aren't changing this, who exactly are we waiting for?

Santa Claus?

This isn't a failure of power. It's a failure of priorities.

A Movement That Fails Quietly

Every time a 16-year-old girl is coerced, pressured, or outright forced into marriage, feminism doesn't just lose—it fails spectacularly. And it's not just about the individual tragedies. The real failure lies in the fact that the *laws* still allow this to happen. That's not some isolated glitch or outdated ideology—it's a current, living reality, sanctioned by the very system feminism claims to challenge.

And where is the uproar? The protests? The viral campaigns? The angry Twitter threads? Nowhere. The silence is deafening.

Maybe it's because these girls don't fit the preferred feminist narrative: they're not CEOs, not influencers, not career-driven powerhouses. They're invisible. They don't have platforms or sponsors. They don't make a compelling Instagram story or a catchy slogan. They are the quiet casualties of a movement that loves the spotlight but shies away from inconvenient truths.

If feminism truly claims to be a movement for *all* women, it needs to show up where it's hardest—where voices are smallest and stakes are highest. Because leaving these girls behind isn't just negligence; it's a betrayal.

So here's the harsh truth: if the movement won't protect those who can't fight for themselves, maybe it's time to stop pretending this is a movement for *all* women. The loudest claims of liberation ring hollow when the most vulnerable are still trapped in systems designed to silence them.

At some point, hashtags and empowerment speeches become meaningless if the laws keep allowing child marriage. If we can't fix this glaring injustice, what have we really achieved?

Feminism must reckon with its failures in silence. Or risk being remembered not as a movement that changed the world, but as one that left the quietest victims behind.

Let's Fix the Damn Law

This isn't rocket science. It's not a complex constitutional dilemma. It's basic decency, wrapped in legal tape and buried under generations of bureaucratic cowardice. And yet, somehow, we still haven't managed to fix it.

Here's what we *don't* need:
Another think piece. Another panel discussion. Another painfully vague "awareness campaign" featuring soft music and vague calls to "do better."

What we *do* need:
A hard legal stop. No marriages under 18. No exceptions. Not if you're in love. Not if your parents say it's okay. Not even if some family friend with a creepy mustache insists it's part of his culture. Eighteen. Period.

Because when the law lets a 40-year-old man marry someone who's in Grade 10, that's not cultural sensitivity. That's state-sanctioned grooming.

And spare us the tired excuses—"But what if they're in love?" "What if it's a religious thing?" "What if the parents approve?" Sorry, no. If your religion or culture involves marrying children, the problem isn't the law—it's your tradition. And if a parent signs off on it, they shouldn't be giving consent. They should be giving a police statement.

There is nothing progressive about keeping legal loopholes open for predators in suits. There's nothing tolerant about tolerating exploitation. And there's nothing "gray area" about a child being married off before she's old enough to vote, drink, or light a cigarette after a moment of intense passion.

So here's a wild idea: Let's stop making excuses and just fix the damn law.

Raise the legal marriage age to 18. No fine print. No "if the parents agree" clause. Just a hard, unapologetic line that says, "We don't marry children in this country."

Because if we can't even agree that a girl should finish high school before becoming someone's wife, someone's property, someone's burden—then maybe we don't get to call ourselves a civilized society.

We can't claim progress while standing on the backs of underage girls in wedding dresses.

Let's fix it—or admit we're fine with it.

Trans Rights vs. Women's Rights?

Biological Women Silenced in the Name of Inclusion

Shelters. Sports. Prisons.

These aren't just spaces—they're lifelines. They were built for biological women who've spent centuries being told to be quiet, to be modest, to stay safe (but not *too* safe), and to smile while doing it. And now, in the name of "progress," we're handing these hard-won sanctuaries over like party favours at a woke birthday bash. Because feelings matter more than biology, right?

What started as a noble march toward equality has detoured into a bureaucratic carnival where reality bends under the weight of hashtags, and "woman" is now a term with asterisked footnotes longer than a pharmaceutical warning label.

Let's get one thing straight: supporting trans people is not the problem. We should all want to live in a world where no one is harassed, beaten, or killed for being who they are. *That's basic decency, not activism.* But here's the plot twist: you don't elevate one group by steamrolling another.

Try saying that on a university campus and watch a Gender Studies major explode like a glitter-filled piñata.

Welcome to Feminism 4.0: Now with Fewer Women!

Modern feminism, bless its self-devouring heart, has become a movement that can't define "woman" without a committee meeting and a crisis of conscience. Somewhere along the way, the cause that fought for suffrage, for equal pay, for bodily autonomy, lost the plot. Now it's too busy managing its optics on social media to notice that the biological women it claims to protect are getting quietly shoved out the back door.

Want to protect women's sports? Bigot.

Prefer rape shelters to remain female-only? Transphobe.

Concerned about male-bodied inmates sharing cells with female prisoners? Fascist.

We went from "Smash the patriarchy" to "Sit down, sweetheart, and let Jessica with the Adam's apple explain what it *really* means to be a woman."

Female Spaces, Male Frames

It's not that shelters, sports teams, and prisons have become "inclusive," it's that they've become battlegrounds. And biological women are losing. Imagine being a trauma survivor seeking refuge from male violence, only to find yourself bunking next to someone who just last month was still using the men's locker room.

Imagine training your whole life as an athlete—counting calories, missing parties, enduring stress fractures—only to be beaten by someone who didn't have to grow breasts or deal with a period at thirteen but still gets to claim the trophy because of "identity."

Call it what you want—equity, compassion, social justice—but if your progress demands that biological women shut up and smile while being sidelined, then your movement isn't justice. It's cosplay with political backing.

When Inclusivity Becomes Absurdity

There's a special kind of irony in watching feminism, a movement founded to defend women, now punish women for *being too womanly*. Do you have uterine cramps? That's not inclusive. Did your pregnancy cause workplace discrimination? Take it up with HR, but maybe don't gender the conversation too hard.

It's as if feminism, in its desperate attempt to be the "cool mom," has invited everyone into the house, given them the master bedroom, and told the daughters to sleep on the floor—and maybe not complain too loud, because they might offend the guests.

The modern feminist response to these concerns usually comes in two flavours:

- "This is a non-issue." (Translation: Shut up.)
- "You're aligning with the far-right." (Translation: STFU.)

Both ignore the very real, very physical, very inconvenient facts about female biology. And when actual women do speak up? They're shunned by the very movement that was supposed to empower them. They're unfriended, unfunded, and uninvited.

So here's a radical idea: maybe feminism should go back to protecting women. All women. Especially the ones with uteruses, XX chromosomes, and a long, bloody history of being told to take up less space.

Because right now, the message being sent is loud and clear: *You can be anything you want—unless that thing is unapologetically female.*

Biology Isn't Bigotry

Let's get one thing straight: recognizing sex differences isn't hate speech. It's called science. Or at least, it *used* to be, before biology got cancelled for being "problematic."

From the moment a child is born—*or better yet, conceived*—biology starts to do its thing. It's not a social construct. It's a chemical one. A chromosomal one. A hormonal one. Boys and girls diverge on two distinct tracks, each with their own milestones, challenges, and landmines. But today, if you dare say that out loud, someone somewhere will light a pronoun flag on fire and call you a TERF.

The Puberty Fork in the Road

For boys, puberty often means a surge of testosterone, broader shoulders, deeper voices, and a social green light to take up space. They're expected to grow into men who win, dominate, and succeed. The worst thing they can be called is "weak"—a word society still conveniently equates with *femininity*.

Girls, on the other hand, get a puberty experience that's less "Rocky montage" and more "Stephen King horror movie."

We're talking cramps, acne, periods, boobs that show up before you're mentally ready—and the sudden awareness that the world is now watching your body like a hawk in heat.

And this biological chaos doesn't come with cheering crowds. It comes with shame. With unsolicited comments. With your value being measured by thigh gaps and cup sizes. You're not just going through changes—you're being *graded* on them.

And if you lose the genetic lottery? Good luck. Society has a whole economy built on making you feel like garbage for not being "hot enough."

But please, tell girls again how *womanhood is just a feeling.*

Health Realities No One Wants to Talk About

Let's get clinical.

- **Endometriosis:** Pain so intense it's mistaken for appendicitis. Often misdiagnosed for years. Still underfunded. Still misunderstood.
- **Polycystic Ovarian Syndrome:** Hormonal hell that affects everything from your weight to your fertility and sanity.
- **Uterine Fibroids. Ovarian Cysts. Infertility. Cervical Cancer:**
  All the charming extras that come with having a uterus, and yet somehow we're told these are

just footnotes in a bigger, more "inclusive" conversation.

Even breast cancer, *now the most diagnosed cancer in the world*, still kills half a million people each year. 99.9% of them are women. But don't worry: we're being very careful not to *gender* the disease too much. Wouldn't want the data to be exclusionary.

These aren't feelings. They're *realities*. They shape the female experience in ways that no amount of lip gloss or gender workshops can replicate. And yet, if you say that out loud today, you risk being branded as a bigot for *acknowledging basic anatomy*.

The Empathy Illusion

We're told, "Just have empathy. Just accept that some people feel like women."

Okay, but empathy isn't a magic key that unlocks someone else's pain. You can empathize with a burn victim without insisting you've been on fire. You can support someone's transition without pretending that estrogen pills rewrite puberty, or that surgical vaginas come with uteruses and lifetime pap smears.

To say otherwise is not compassion—it's delusion, weaponized.

And it's not just delusional. It's dangerous. Because when biology is no longer allowed to matter in medicine, in data, in public policy, women lose. They lose protection, they lose services, and they lose voice.

If that's what "progress" looks like, then it's walking in heels it didn't earn.

This Isn't Bigotry. It's Boundaries.

We don't have to sacrifice truth to be kind. And we don't have to destroy women to validate someone else's identity.

Saying "women face specific, lifelong, biological realities" isn't exclusionary. It's *reality*.

And no amount of progressive platitudes can bleed for you once a month, deliver a child, or fight off a gynecological cancer.

You can call that bigotry if you want.

But maybe—just maybe—it's called being female.

When Compassion Becomes Erasure

Let's be clear from the start: this is not an attack on trans people. This is not a crusade to deny anyone's dignity or humanity. In fact, it's quite the opposite—because when a movement that claims to support women starts demanding their silence, someone has to ask the uncomfortable questions.

Yes, trans women face discrimination. Yes, they often live at the margins of society. Yes, they deserve protection.

But here's the problem: when "compassion" demands that biological women erase their boundaries, deny their biology, and give up the very spaces built for their safety, then compassion has mutated into something else entirely.

It becomes erasure with lipstick and a Twitter handle.

The Slogan That Silences

"Trans women are women."
We've all heard it. It's repeated like scripture, usually followed by a threat of cancellation if you so much as blink too slowly. On the surface, it sounds kind. It's meant to affirm identity, offer belonging. But here's the inconvenient truth:

Slogans aren't science.

And identity is not anatomy.

A person born male, raised male, and who went through male puberty carries a biological legacy that can't be cancelled with hormones or hashtags. Broader shoulders, denser bones, bigger lungs, higher muscle mass—these aren't social constructs. They're performance enhancers handed out by Mother Nature herself.

This is why, when biological males start competing in women's sports, the records start falling like drunk toddlers.

We're watching decades of women's athletic history be rewritten—not by better training or talent, but by biology bulldozing fairness in the name of "inclusion."

And when women speak up? They're vilified. Told to shut up. Told they're "TERFs," bigots, Nazis—take your pick.

Welcome to modern feminism, where you're allowed to talk about your period on stage but not your fear of being physically overpowered by someone with a different skeletal structure.

The Politics of Safety

Let's leave the track field and step into something darker—shelters and prisons.

These aren't just "spaces." These are sanctuaries—places women go when they've been beaten, raped, or robbed a bank. Places where they're finally supposed to feel safe from being assaulted by men.

But thanks to an overzealous interpretation of gender inclusivity, biological males are now being placed in women's shelters and female prisons simply by self-identifying as women. No surgery required. No transition needed. Just words.

And what happens next? Exactly what you'd expect—except no one wants to talk about it.

There have been assaults. There have been pregnancies. There have been traumatized women forced to relive their worst nightmares, not because of an accident or oversight, but because of policy. Because someone thought "inclusion" was more important than trauma-informed care.

Women who dare to object—many of them survivors of sexual violence—are told to "educate themselves." Told they're being hateful. Imagine escaping a man who painfully diddled you, only to be locked in a room with someone who still has the same anatomy.

And then being told you're the problem.

That's not feminism.

That's abuse with pronouns.

When Feminism Forgets Women

Modern feminism seems to have taken a detour. Once a movement rooted in empowering women based on shared female experience, it now spends more time debating who gets to *define* womanhood than fighting for the material rights of women themselves.

The result? A generation of young girls who are being taught that saying "I feel like a woman" is the same as growing up as one.

But womanhood isn't a costume. It's not makeup, curves, or a sense of softness. It's not a TikTok filter. It's a lifelong biological and social experience, complete with periods, hormones, fertility battles, breast cancer, and the terrifying reality that most violence against women is still committed by men.

That's not identity.

That's biology, history, and survival.

And yet, somehow, saying this out loud makes you the villain.

The Right to Say "No"

Women have every right to be kind. But they also have every right to set boundaries without being labelled cruel.

They can support trans rights without surrendering their own.

They can fight for dignity for everyone without agreeing to be erased in the process.

It's not bigotry to say that spaces built for women should remain female-only when biology is what those spaces are meant to address.

It's not hate to say, "I want fairness in sport, safety in shelters, and truth in language."

It's common sense.

And we're running out of it.

Kindness Doesn't Require Blindness

Inclusion should never be a zero-sum game, but increasingly it feels like one. Because when women are told their needs, biology, and fears must be hidden so others can feel seen, that's not justice. That's gaslighting.

Compassion doesn't require women to lie.

It doesn't require them to be silent.

And it damn sure doesn't require them to give up the only protections they've ever had in the name of a progressive fairy tale.

So call it what it is: erasure, not equality.

Because a feminism that forgets women isn't feminism at all.

Protecting One Doesn't Mean Erasing Another

Here's a revolutionary idea in the era of emotional landmines and social media pile-ons: you can support trans rights *and* defend women's spaces at the same time. Wild, right? Turns out, this isn't a branding war between hashtags—it's a real-world clash over biology, safety, dignity, and the right to boundaries.

When women fight to preserve women's sports, it's not because they're transphobic or insecure about their biceps. It's because they understand a simple fact: testosterone-fuelled adolescence leaves behind more than chest hair. It leaves behind structural advantages that don't melt away with hormones and a name change.

When women raise hell over biological males in female prisons, shelters, or locker rooms, they're not gatekeeping femininity—they're trying to avoid getting shoved into trauma therapy for the third time.

But here's the kicker: even trans men—people assigned female at birth—get it. They still bleed, still face the risks of pregnancy, breast cancer, and all the joy that comes with having a uterus in a world that seems to think your pain is "part of the magic." Most of them don't pretend they've escaped the baggage of being born female just because they've grown some stubble and changed their license.

So, if trans men can acknowledge they carry the physical weight of being born female...

Why are trans women somehow allowed to rewrite the entire definition of what a woman is?

We're not talking about feelings here—we're talking about organs, trauma patterns, and risks unique to female biology. You can't opt into that. You don't just pick "woman" off a shelf like you're shopping for gender at Walmart.

Being a woman isn't about eyeliner or empathy. It's about surviving a world that has historically preyed on your body, your fertility, your vulnerability. It's not a costume. It's not a role you play on TikTok. And it's definitely not something you validate by silencing the women who've lived it since birth.

This isn't about exclusion. It's about survival. And any movement that demands one group erase their reality so another can feel more affirmed is no longer about equality—it's about power. And women have spent millennia being on the losing end of that equation.

So no, we're not going back.

Not quietly.

Not ever.

This Isn't a Slogan

Motherhood. Menstruation. Menopause.
These aren't vibes. They're not trends. They're not something you cosplay on the internet and then log out of when it gets uncomfortable. They are blood-and-bone realities—equal parts joy, agony, and unpredictability. You don't get stretch marks or hot flashes from identifying. You get them from living.

This isn't a dig at trans women. No one's saying they don't deserve respect. But when we start erasing biological distinctions to soothe feelings, we're not building bridges—we're digging mass graves for truth. And buried right next to it? Every hard-won gain women fought for over decades.

The irony? Feminism, the movement meant to liberate women, is now gaslighting them in the name of progress. Say "women give birth," and suddenly you're problematic. Mention that cervical cancer screenings are a female issue, and you're branded a bigot. All this in a culture that throws around "follow the science" like it's a commandment—except, of course, when the science makes someone uncomfortable.

Let's be crystal clear:

Supporting trans people does not require lying about biology.

And being a woman should not come with a gag order.

It's entirely possible to fight for everyone's dignity without pretending we're all carbon copies in different outfits. We're not. Women's bodies are different. Women's risks are different. Women's needs are different.

That's not hateful. That's not exclusionary.

That's just biology.

So, if your feminism demands women shut up for someone else to feel seen, congratulations, you're not a feminist. You're a rebranded misogynist with better hashtags.

Let's build a world where everyone is safe—yes.

But let's stop pretending we're all the same.

We're not. And that's okay.

What's not okay is punishing women for daring to say so out loud.

Somewhere along the line, feminism lost the plot.

What began as a movement to liberate women from silence, submission, and second-class status has morphed into something unrecognizable—a stage where biological women are expected to play background extras in their own story. Spaces once carved out for their safety, dignity, and health are now battlegrounds for ideological purity tests. Say the wrong thing, acknowledge biology, or, God forbid, mention menstruation, and suddenly you're a heretic.

We were told feminism was about choice, truth, and protecting the vulnerable. But today, truth is negotiable, choice must be politically correct, and the vulnerable—namely, women in prisons, shelters, and sports—are told to shut up and stop being so "exclusionary." When did feminism start punching down?

This chapter has laid it bare: biology isn't bigotry. Acknowledging that male puberty confers physical advantages isn't hateful—it's honest. Saying that periods, pregnancy, and menopause are exclusive to female bodies isn't erasure—it's reality. And demanding safety and fairness in women's spaces isn't cruelty—it's survival.

We can—and should—support trans people. We can show compassion, push for dignity, and fight discrimination. But compassion without boundaries becomes erasure. Inclusion, when weaponized, stops being noble and starts being oppressive.

If feminism no longer has room for the word "woman," then who, exactly, is it for?

This chapter isn't a call to hate. It's a call to stop pretending. To reclaim the movement before it becomes another ideology that demands silence instead of change. Protecting biological women isn't an act of war—it's the bare minimum. Because if feminism won't defend women, then what's left to believe in?

Empowered to Stay Silent

The phrase *"Believe all women"* was originally meant to address the cultural tendency to dismiss women's claims of harassment or abuse. It was a reaction to decades—if not centuries—of disbelief, victim-blaming, and institutional silence. But somewhere along the way, the phrase was hijacked. It morphed from a call for justice into an unconditional rallying cry—*believe all women... as long as they're saying what we want to hear.*

The Unspoken Conditions of Belief

Modern feminism says it wants to amplify women's voices. But that comes with fine print:

- Agree with progressive politics? You're brave.
- Vote right-of-center, question gender ideology, or say you prefer family over career? Suddenly, you're not to be taken seriously.

Ask Tara Reade. She accused a beloved high-powered left-wing politician of sexual assault, and the feminist establishment turned into a ghost town. No marches. No hashtags. No late-night monologues. Just silence, skepticism, and in some corners, outright mockery.

The message is clear: *You are only credible if your pain is politically convenient.*

The Hypocrisy of Empowerment

Disagree with modern feminism, and you're not just wrong—you're disqualified from womanhood itself.

- Stay-at-home mom? You've internalized oppression.
- Proudly feminine? You're playing into the male gaze.
- Religious? You've been indoctrinated.
- Conservative? You're not even *really* a woman, just a tool of the patriarchy.

The ideological gatekeeping is so tight, you could bounce a coin off it. And if you try to speak out? You're shouted down by women who claim to speak for you.

Language as a Weapon

The labels come fast and sharp:

- *Pick-me*
- *Tradwife*
- *Handmaid*
- *Anti-woman*

All of these are designed to shame dissent into silence. Feminism, which once claimed to fight for choice, now seems to only tolerate a *very specific kind* of choice—the one that aligns with its politics and aesthetics.

It's not enough to be a woman. You must be the *right kind* of woman.

When "Belief" Becomes a Sledgehammer

The phrase *"Believe all women"* has also lost its nuance. It no longer implies *listen, investigate, and take seriously.* Instead, it's become a loyalty test—a way to prove you're on the right side. And loyalty means unquestioning support for certain narratives, not others.

This double standard not only hurts individual women, but it also undermines the credibility of the entire movement. If feminism will only "believe" some women, then it isn't about belief. It's tribalism.

Tradition Isn't Treason

Feminism once promised women freedom—the freedom to choose their paths, whether that meant raising children, running companies, or doing both. But today, that promise feels hollow for women who don't want to climb a corporate ladder or burn bras in the town square. For them, *"choice"* has become conditional. Their version of womanhood is no longer just unfashionable—it's unforgivable.

The Rebranding of Oppression

Stay-at-home mothers are told they've surrendered their potential.

Modest dressers are pitied as repressed.

Religious women are mocked for their "fairy tales."

Traditional wives are labelled as oppressed, brainwashed, or dangerous.

But who decided that caregiving, faith, and femininity were signs of weakness? The irony is rich: a movement born to shatter stereotypes has built an entirely new cage—this time lined with LinkedIn profiles, ideological purity, and endless career ambition. If your fulfillment doesn't come from a paycheck or a podium, you're seen as setting women back.

"The Wrong Kind" of Empowerment

The woman who stays home to raise her kids is often more vilified than the man who leaves his. And why? Because she chose something that doesn't fit the modern narrative. She didn't "lean in," she leaned into what mattered to her. And for that, she's considered a traitor to her gender.

Online spaces that claim to uplift women are often where these traditional women are bullied the most. They're called:

- *Anti-feminist*
- *Internalized misogynists*
- *Pick-mes*
- *Tradcults*

These aren't just insults—they're attempts to delegitimize women's autonomy under the guise of defending it.

Choice Means *All* Choices

If feminism only celebrates women who live like men, is it really about women at all? When ambition is praised but nurturing is ridiculed, we haven't progressed—we've just changed the uniform. The truth is, many traditional women are deeply intelligent, fully capable, and entirely conscious of their decisions. They're not victims. They're not mindless. And they don't need saving.

Respecting women means respecting *all* women, including the ones who choose paths that look "backward" to others. Freedom isn't freedom if you're punished for using it the "wrong" way.

Mob Rule, Not Sisterhood

Online feminism has traded sisterhood for surveillance, solidarity for silencing. What once aimed to liberate has mutated into a purity cult where deviation is a punishable offence and dissent is met with digital exile.

Speak out—say that biology matters, that motherhood is meaningful, or that not all women see men as oppressors—and watch the algorithm light up like a witch trial. You're branded a *traitor*, a *bigot*, a *handmaiden of the patriarchy*. Forget dialogue. Forget nuance. You're not debated—you're destroyed.

The Thought Police Wear Pink Now

You can be a woman. You can be smart. But if you're not a woman in the *correct way*, you're the enemy.

If you say "sex is real"—cancelled.

If you express doubts about gender ideology—cancelled.

If you question feminist orthodoxy on motherhood or femininity—cancelled.

Your career? Fair game.

Your safety? Irrelevant.

Your voice? A threat.

These aren't fringe reactions—they're the norm in digital feminism. And the enforcers aren't men in power suits; they're women with hashtags, weaponized narratives, and burner accounts. Mob rule, dressed up as moral clarity.

Weaponized Wokeness

What began as a movement for equality has become a tribunal for ideological compliance. You're either fully in—or fully erased. And what's worse, the mob doesn't go after institutions of power. It goes after *women*. Real women. Mothers. Immigrants. Survivors. Anyone who steps off-script. Because control, not compassion, is the new cornerstone.

This isn't feminism. It's fear-based conformity with a soft-glow filter.

Politics Over Principles

Feminist outrage today doesn't hinge on what's done—it hinges on *who* did it. The same behaviour that sparks a social media inferno when committed by someone on the right barely registers a flicker when it comes from the left.

A conservative man tells an off-colour joke? Cancel him. Fire him. Dox him.

A progressive darling is caught groping women at a fundraiser? He's "evolving." Let's "have grace."

The rules aren't rules—they're weapons. And justice isn't blind anymore; she's squinting through partisan glasses.

Selective Empathy

Even female victims aren't treated equally.

If a right-leaning woman comes forward with abuse allegations, she's scrutinized, shamed, or outright ignored. Wrong politics, wrong victim. But if the woman is a feminist icon or progressive activist? She's believed before she even speaks.

Truth doesn't matter. The narrative does.

And if your truth threatens the movement's image, it gets buried under hashtags and talking points.

Power Over Protection

This isn't about protecting women. It's about protecting *the brand*.

That's why male feminist allies get infinite second chances—because they say the right things. And why women who choose faith, family, or conservative values are tossed aside, because they *don't*.

Feminism, at its worst, has become less about equality and more about tribal loyalty. Principles take a back seat to political positioning. And the result? A movement that claims to empower women, while weaponizing their pain for power plays.

Third World Women? Sorry, No Wi-Fi, No Clout

There's a whole world out there where being a woman is still a matter of survival. Where girls are married before puberty. Where rape victims are jailed. Where education is a luxury and menstruation is a curse. But scroll through mainstream feminist platforms and you'd never know.

Why?

Because these stories don't trend.

Western feminism has become addicted to optics—easy outrage, glossy activism, and causes that come with filters and hashtags. It's hard to posture about smashing the patriarchy when you're confronted with girls who are literally chained to it. It's harder still to turn those stories into viral soundbites or profitable slogans.

So they're ignored.

No press tours. No walkouts. No profile pic overlays. Just silence—because these women can't retweet your think-piece. They can't buy your feminist subscription box. And they certainly can't help you land a book deal.

Feminism, but Make It Marketable

We don't need more TED Talks about "finding your voice" from women who've never lost theirs.

We need action—real, dirty, unfiltered, on-the-ground action—for those who have none.

But modern feminism doesn't scale well across suffering it can't monetize. The pain of brown girls in war zones doesn't pair nicely with influencer aesthetics. And that's the point. Today's feminism isn't a global sisterhood. It's a boutique movement with a Wi-Fi password.

Feminism for the Few

The bitter truth? Feminism, as practiced today, doesn't advocate for all women. It advocates for a very specific kind: urban, educated, politically left, ambitious—but only in approved ways. Step outside that mould, and you're not seen as empowered. You're seen as a threat.

It's not a movement anymore—it's a marketing strategy with a victimhood clause. A polished brand, curated for social media, designed to elevate a few while silencing the rest.

It's not about justice. It's about optics.

It's not about freedom. It's about compliance.

And it's certainly not about women as a whole, just the ones who know how to play the game.

Because in today's feminist playbook, it's not enough to be a woman. You have to be the *right* kind of woman.

And that, more than anything, is the betrayal.

Who Actually Benefits?

The Business of Feminism: Selling Hope, Banking on Fear

Feminism used to be a cause. Now, for many, it's a career.

Behind every hashtag and headline, there's a price tag—and increasingly, that tag is being cashed in by those who've figured out the perfect formula: a compelling message of empowerment, a desperate audience in pain, and a system that rewards virality over virtue.

Enter the modern feminist nonprofit-industrial complex.

From NGOs to influencer-led campaigns, feminism has become a lucrative brand. Organize a march, slap a slogan on a tote bag, get a few thousand followers—and suddenly, you're marketable. Corporations take notice. Governments offer grants. Media platforms amplify your voice. But the women who truly need help? They're still struggling, still unseen, and still excluded from the wealth flowing behind the scenes.

Hope as a Hook, Fear as Fuel

Modern feminism has figured out something crucial: desperate women make loyal followers. Women battling low self-esteem, trauma, discrimination, or isolation become prime targets for saviour messaging. Want to feel seen? Validated? Safe? Just follow, subscribe, attend, donate, and don't ask too many questions about where the money goes.

It's the oldest sales trick in the book: create a problem, sell the solution. Or better yet, exaggerate the problem and sell *yourself* as the solution.

Want proof? Let's follow the money.

Receipts, Not Rhetoric: Feminism's Monetized Machinery

1. The $500,000 March T-Shirt

Remember the *Women's March* in 2017? It was supposed to be a historic moment of global solidarity. And it was—until the co-founders started feuding over money, power, and press access like they were auditioning for a feminist reboot of *Succession*. Meanwhile, grassroots organizers got nothing but sunburns and Instagram likes.

Moral of the story: Revolution, but make it marketable.

2. Girlboss or Just Bossy?

Sophia Amoruso made "#GIRLBOSS" the holy grail of feminist ambition. Her book, podcast, and Netflix series taught millions how to hustle. But inside her company, Nasty Gal, employees, especially women of colour, accused her of being anything *but* empowering. Allegations of discrimination and union-busting soured the brand. Turns out, the girlboss wasn't fighting the patriarchy. She *was* the patriarchy, just in lipstick.

3. TEDx, Trauma, and Tiaras

Some feminist influencers have mastered the art of turning personal pain into premium content. You don't need credentials—just a tragic story and a ring light. Slap together a TEDx talk about "Reclaiming Space" and suddenly you're a thought leader. Meanwhile, the actual women fighting systemic abuse in Congo or India are still begging for menstrual pads and access to school.

If your feminism doesn't have a press kit, is it even real?

4. Woke Washing 101

Gillette scored PR points with its "toxic masculinity" ad campaign. Very progressive. Empowering, even. Until you learn that their parent company, Procter &

Gamble, profits from skin-lightening creams in Southeast Asia. Because nothing says equality like telling dark-skinned women to lighten up—literally.

5. NGO = Networking Grifters Only

Let's talk numbers. A well-known European charity received millions in funding to fight gender-based violence. Less than 12% went to actual survivors. The rest? Office rent, consultant fees, branded folders, and "awareness workshops" held in boutique hotels. Because clearly, feminism is best discussed over $18 quinoa bowls.

6. Influencer Priestesses and the Gospel of Trauma

If you've ever watched a woman cry on TikTok while promoting a $999 healing course, congratulations, you've seen the Holy Grail of trauma capitalism. These InstaFeminists peddle spiritual recovery, "divine feminine" awakenings, and emotional labour coaching—all while crying in HD. The sadder the reel, the steeper the fee. Refunds? Never. Healing? Optional.

Who's Benefiting? (Spoiler: Not the Women You Think)

The truth is, for every woman spending hours under the sun chanting for justice, there's someone sitting in an air-conditioned office writing grant proposals in her name. The money doesn't trickle down to single mothers, survivors of domestic abuse, or girls denied education. It stops at the top, lining the pockets of those who've turned empowerment into an enterprise.

And sometimes, there's a man behind the curtain—a PR-savvy executive who realized he could just hire a few charismatic women to front his NGO or company, watch them pull in the followers, and enjoy the ROI. It's capitalism 101: outsource your marketing, collect your millions.

The Psychology Behind It All

This machine runs on a simple principle: sympathetic presence after emotional trauma. If you can scare women enough—tell them most men are monsters, tell them that forgetting your birthday is a form of abuse—you create a psychological opening. Into that vacuum of fear and loneliness, the modern feminist entrepreneur walks in, ready to sell hope at a markup.

The women buying in aren't stupid. They're just exhausted. When your life is crumbling, sometimes a good slogan is enough. Sometimes, just being seen—even if it's by someone selling empowerment candles—is more than you've ever had. That's how they get you. And that's how they keep you.

Feminism for the Few

The bitter truth? Feminism, as practiced today, doesn't advocate for all women. It advocates for a very specific kind: urban, educated, politically left, ambitious—but only in approved ways. It's not a movement anymore—it's a marketing strategy with a victimhood clause.

It's not about justice. It's about optics.

It's not about freedom. It's about compliance.

And it's certainly not about *women as a whole*, just the ones who know how to play the game.

So the next time you see a "feminist" conference hosted at a luxury hotel, with a $300 entrance fee and sponsored by a perfume brand, ask yourself who it's really for. Because if feminism were truly about liberation, more women would be free.

Instead, they're just... following.

Panels, Conferences, and Clout

At the top of the feminist industrial pyramid are the crowned queens of clout: TEDx speakers, panel moderators, Instagram gurus with ring lights and publicists. These are the "leaders"—the ones who speak of glass ceilings while sipping sparkling water in five-star hotel ballrooms. They lament oppression from front-row seats at fashion week and deliver keynote addresses about inclusivity, at $3,000 a pop.

It's feminism as spectacle. Feminism as a career.

They don't break the system—they brand it.

Meanwhile, the working-class women—single mothers, refugee girls, domestic abuse survivors, cashiers pulling doubles—don't get platforms. They get *slogans*. They get "You Go Girl" stickers and tote bags with "Boss Babe" printed in faux gold. They're told they're "empowered" as long as they retweet the right influencer, donate to the right GoFundMe, or wear pink to the march.

Empowerment, for them, isn't a lived experience—it's a performance for someone else's profit.

Because behind every "awareness" campaign is a sponsorship deal. Behind every viral march is an email blast promising "collaboration opportunities." Every time a woman signs up to volunteer, a small circle of elites are negotiating ad space. Every time someone donates $20 to "support survivors," an "activist" is collecting a speaker's fee and checking into a boutique hotel for a panel titled *"Healing in the Age of Hashtags."*

This isn't activism. It's marketing.

And just like any good marketing campaign, it's all about audience retention. Keep women loyal, scared, angry, hopeful. Feed them trauma, sprinkle in empowerment, and upsell the next seminar, the next e-course, the next merch drop. Make them believe the movement is for them, while making sure the profits stay at the top.

In the church of modern feminism, the pews are full of struggling women. The pulpit? Reserved for those with brand deals and a well-filtered sob story.

Desperation Sells

There's a reason modern feminism spreads fastest among the disillusioned, the depressed, and the desperate—it's not because they're weak. It's because they're searching for *something*. Hope, belonging, validation. When someone is emotionally worn down or feels invisible, even a half-baked TED quote wrapped in pastel colours can feel like gospel.

Feminist branding knows this.

And like all great marketers, it sells *solutions* to problems it helped spotlight—sometimes even *create*.

It starts with trauma inflation. Overblown stats, cherry-picked horror stories, and social media campaigns that make you feel like the world is a dystopian hellscape run entirely by cartoon villains in cargo shorts. It floods timelines with oppression, heartbreak, and "Did you know 97% of women..." graphics designed to scare first and ask questions never.

Then it slips in the pitch:

Buy the shirt.

Join the movement.

Donate today.

It's the oldest trick in the capitalist playbook: manufacture a need, sell the fix, rinse, repeat. If a woman is already cracked by society, a movement that promises healing, even if symbolic, feels like salvation. Who has time to verify data when you're crying in your car after a 12-hour shift and a cancelled daycare slot?

And sure, some of the trauma is very real. But the "solutions" usually aren't. A march doesn't pay rent. A podcast about "breaking cycles" won't keep your abuser away. A T-shirt that says "FEMINIST AF" doesn't come with childcare. These symbolic gestures are good for one thing: *raising awareness*. That's marketing code for "looking like we're doing something while actually doing nothing."

Meanwhile, the heavy lifting—housing, therapy, job training, protection—is left to crumbling public programs and overworked social workers. The same women who get paraded around as examples of "why we fight" are promptly ignored when the checks get written.

But here's the kicker: if a feminist cause isn't profitable, it disappears like last season's handbag.

Women facing child marriage in Sudan? Girls banned from school in Afghanistan? Victims of FGM in Somalia? Sorry, no aesthetic. No catchy hashtag. No corporate partnership potential. You can't slap that on a water bottle and sell it at Urban Outfitters.

Because real suffering doesn't look good on Instagram.

And real change?

That doesn't sell nearly as well as stickers.

Follow the Money

Here's the punchline: a lot of these feminist "movements" aren't even run by women.
They're funded by men—very rich, very strategic men—who looked at the gender struggle and saw not a moral imperative, but a *market opportunity*.

Want to cash in on the empowerment economy? Easy.

Set up a nonprofit, throw in a few well-lit photos of crying women, add some trauma buzzwords, and find a charismatic female spokesperson to sell it. Boom. Feminism-as-a-Service is live.

Behind every pastel Instagram grid, there's a boardroom full of men in Patagonia vests asking, *"So, how do we monetize gender equity this quarter?"* And the answer is always the same: *hire a few women to look passionate on camera and make sure the donation button works.*

This isn't a conspiracy—it's a business model.

The structure is a classic pyramid scheme: at the top, the founders—often white, often male, always loaded. Then come the visible figureheads: the TEDx speakers, the authors with blurry photos of their crying 12-year-old selves on book covers, the "activist entrepreneurs" with media kits. Below them, the mid-level motivators: the panel hosts, workshop leaders, the Instagram therapists with $200 trauma-healing bootcamps.

And at the very bottom?

The volunteers. The marchers. The ones who set up chairs, write personal essays for exposure, and staff hotline shifts for free.

They're told they're part of a movement.

What they're actually part of is a marketing funnel.

Because the closer you are to the actual suffering, the less money there is.

The farther you get from the trauma, up through the layers of consultants, brand managers, and "thought leaders," the bigger the paychecks.

Even the term "grassroots" has become a branding tool. If your suffering can't be distilled into an aesthetic carousel post or turned into a compelling grant application? You're not marketable. You're a liability.

So while single moms juggle night shifts and survival, someone's buying their third home off a bestselling memoir about *radical softness.* And while you're reposting quotes about reclaiming your power, someone's quietly reclaiming your wallet.

The only glass ceiling many of these organizations are breaking is the one on their office champagne flutes.

Trauma as a Sales Funnel

It's not just storytelling. It's salesmanship—with trauma as the pitch.

Psychologically, people coming out of trauma crave understanding. They're not looking for Harvard degrees; they're looking for someone who gets it. Enter the modern feminist influencer: not a trained therapist, not a policy expert—just a "survivor" with a ring light, a tearful backstory (real or borrowed), and a monetized comment section.

You don't need credentials when you have vibes.

And trauma, it turns out, is a goldmine for vibe-based marketing.

The formula is simple:

Stir pain, exaggerate villains, and position yourself as a healer.

So you get things like:

- "All men are trash" (2M likes)
- "If he forgot your birthday, he's an abuser" (3M shares)
- "Challenging your opinion is emotional violence" (now available as a mug for $18.99)

These sound unhinged to the stable. But they land like gospel to the broken. Not because women are dumb, but because desperation makes even obvious disinformation feel like gospel.

And once the fear is planted? You monetize the solution.

"Join my 6-week trauma recovery circle."

"Subscribe to my $9.99/month healing journey."

"Buy my downloadable eBook on how to leave toxic men (and maybe your dad, too)."

It's not just content—it's customer acquisition. Each reel of righteous rage, each tear-soaked podcast episode, is part of a sales funnel. And trauma is the entry point.

Behind the healing language and glittery graphics, there's always a CTA:

Click. Donate. Subscribe. Believe. Buy.

The grift is simple: build a loyal audience by validating pain, then convert that pain into income.

After all, what is healing if not a brand opportunity?

Feminism, Inc.

This isn't a conspiracy. It's just capitalism with a blow-dried conscience.

Feminism didn't die—it pivoted. It scaled. It rebranded. And like every good business, it found a way to turn pain into profit. Somewhere along the line, "smash the patriarchy" got a trademark symbol. Now it's a hoodie. A curated feed. A corporate partnership with a makeup brand that still doesn't pay garment workers a living wage.

This is Feminism, Inc.
A sleek, scalable enterprise with tiered marketing funnels, KPIs, and crisis-response PR teams. The mission statement? "Empowerment—just $39.99 plus shipping."

Like any successful product, feminism needed a target demographic. Vulnerable women? Check. Collective rage? Check. Universal anxiety about safety, worth, and identity? Bingo. And like every marketing masterclass will tell you: if the demand doesn't exist, create it.

The formula is ancient: stir fear, sprinkle hope, then sell the cure.

Some women at the top think they're helping. That's the truly bleak part. You can only gaslight the world once you've perfected the art on yourself. They wear the right pins, use the right hashtags, speak at the right conferences, and believe that doing so equals revolution. It doesn't. It's just an extremely aesthetic résumé.

Others? They're fully in on the hustle. They know exactly what they're doing—and they're cashing out fast, before the cultural tide shifts. You'll find them sipping sponsored matcha in Bali, posting about "trauma-informed branding" from their influencer retreats. They're not worried about systemic change. They're worried about engagement metrics.

Behind the scenes, brand deals are negotiated. Speaking fees are invoiced. Even tears are scheduled—there's a market for performative breakdowns now, as long as they're captioned with something poetic and vaguely feminist.

"Healing is not linear," she writes, before boarding a business class flight funded by donations.

And if you dare question the ethics? You're accused of internalized misogyny, of being anti-woman, of not supporting "the movement." But what movement?

The only thing moving is the money—from your pocket to theirs.

Because this isn't a conspiracy.

It's just the free market, dressed in activism's clothes.

And in a world where oppression pays, the last thing anyone in power wants is equality.

They'd lose their business model.

Let Men Help

Men Are Not the Enemy. Stop Pretending They Are.

Once upon a time, feminism had a useful story: men were the oppressors, women were the oppressed, and burning your bra was the first step toward liberation. Like most origin stories, it had some truth to it. And like most things marinated in trauma and outrage, it curdled with age, like milk in a heatwave.

Fast-forward to today, and you'll still find a vocal wing of the movement clinging to that 1970s narrative like a moth to a lava lamp. To them, men didn't just build the system—they built it to dominate. End of story. It's a neat, emotionally gratifying plot: clear villains, clean lines, a rotating cast of hashtags. But real life doesn't read like a Tumblr thread. The world is messier. The truth is blurrier. And sometimes, the people holding up the structure are the very ones you've labelled the enemy.

The System That Binds... Is Also Run by Men (Ironically)

Let's talk about *the system.* You know, the one that locks up rapists, chases down abusers, and occasionally ruins a man's life *for good reason?* Guess who's operating it?

The judge handing down a 15-year sentence for sexual assault? Probably a man.

The officer arresting that guy mid-chokehold? Also, a man.

The lawmakers who created the sentencing guidelines? Mostly men. Some bald. Some boring. But not exactly your enemy.

These are not patriarchs in shining armour. They are men with skin in the game. Men who act not to *save* women, but to *stand beside* them.

Protection ≠ Oppression (Stop Twisting It)

Here's another inconvenient truth for the bumper-sticker feminists: a lot of those old "oppressive" laws weren't written out of malice. They were written out of fear. Fear for women's lives in eras when life expectancy was basically "don't get kidnapped."

Picture it: You're a dad in 1300. No phones. No police. Just Viking raids, plague, and open terrain. Of course, you'd restrict your daughter's movement. You wouldn't call it oppression. You'd call it *keeping her alive.*

Even in the 1940s, when the war vacuumed up every man under 40, society didn't say, "Let's empower women!" They said, "Let's not fall apart." The world wasn't ready for equality—it was too busy trying not to collapse.

Those old systems were like bunkers. Crude, protective, and temporary.

Now? We're living in the suburbs. Bike lanes. Lattes. Podcasts.

And yet... some are still screaming, "LOCK THE DOORS!"

Men Are Listening—Even If You're Too Angry to Notice

Here's what you won't hear on feminist TikTok: men have evolved. Quietly. Often painfully.

They've held their wives through miscarriages and watched them fight postpartum depression in silence.

They've heard their daughters come home crying because the internet said they were ugly at age eleven.

They've mentored female coworkers. They've hired, promoted, trained, and supported. Not out of guilt, but out of growth.

And yes, some men learned the hard way—by being called out, dragged, dumped, and demoted.

Others learned by listening. And now they want in—not to lead, not to lecture—but to build.

Yet feminism, in all its ironic glory, continues to dunk on them like they're frat boys in a '90s rom-com.

You want men to help dismantle the system, but you keep calling them the system.

You want collaboration, but treat them like contaminants.

How exactly is that supposed to work?

Stop Selling Rage. Start Building Coalitions.

Here's the truth no one profits from: the men most capable of changing the system are the ones you're currently alienating.

The decent ones. The smart ones. The ones in positions of power who are just waiting for permission to use it for something good. But you've made them afraid to speak.

You mock them when they show emotion.

You silence them when they ask questions.

You shame them when they offer help, as if empathy is mansplaining with a nice tone.

Feminism wasn't supposed to become a religion of resentment. It was meant to be a call to dignity, equality, and yes, partnership. But somewhere between the hashtags and the hot takes, feminists lost the plot.

Let Them Help—Or Be Prepared to Build Alone

Letting men help doesn't mean giving them control.

It means giving them credit when they do the right thing.

It means accepting allies, even if they don't speak your language perfectly.

It means trusting intentions, not just performance.

Because here's the final irony: If the patriarchy really is a fortress, why would you reject the men trying to hand you the keys?

Let them help. Not because they're heroes. But because they're human.

And because if equality is the goal, then *fighting everyone with a penis* is probably not the strategy that gets us there.

Not All Feminists Are the Same

Once upon a time, calling yourself a feminist meant something clean: *equal rights for women.* Mic drop. Applause. Job well done. But like every well-meaning movement, feminism went through puberty—and now it's a hormonal mess with identity issues, shouting matches, and four competing versions of itself all fighting over the same Instagram handle.

You've met them. You've side-eyed their tweets. You've probably ghosted them in a group chat. So let's break them down.

1. The Man-Haters

They don't want equality. They want revenge—and attention.

These are the folks who think feminism is just rage in eyeliner. Their worldview is simple: if it has a Y chromosome, it's guilty. And if you disagree, *you're internalizing patriarchy,* sis.

They don't want men to understand women. They want men to shut up, sit down, and preferably dissolve into ash. You could bring them a male nurse who survived abuse and now volunteers at a women's shelter. They'd still squint and say, "Suspicious."

But they're not just torching men—they're nuking empathy. Try telling them you love your dad. That your brother's your best friend. That your husband cooks, and cries, and shows up. They'll look at you like you just confessed to war crimes.

These people aren't building a movement. They're building a moat—and daring anyone with a penis to cross it.

2. The Martyr Queens

Suffering is their love language. Just don't ask them to heal.

These women collect trauma like vintage handbags. Every wound, every insult, every societal slight? Archived. Alphabetized. Weaponized.

To them, pain isn't something to overcome—it's your entire personality. If you talk about hope, you're naïve. If you mention forgiveness, you're brainwashed. And if you suggest men might also suffer? Prepare for side-eyes that could peel paint.

Ask them about male suicide. "Not our issue."

About boys being medicated for normal behaviour? "Sounds like a you problem."

But here's the dark joke: they're not just ignoring male suffering—they're gatekeeping victimhood. As if empathy is a zero-sum game, and anyone else's pain dilutes their moral currency.

Spoiler: Real feminism isn't a misery contest. You don't need to bleed the most to lead.

3. The Top-10% Chasers

"Smash the patriarchy!" they yell from a boardroom in Louboutins.

This crew doesn't want equality. They want *executive equity* with a corner office view.

They're laser-focused on rich white male power and determined to replicate it, just with a better skincare routine. They say, "We want what men have!" but what they really mean is, "We want what *elite* men have." The yachts. The buyouts. The Forbes 30-under-30 write-ups.

Meanwhile, they ghost the reality that most men aren't flying private—they're fixing HVAC systems or driving Ubers so their kids can eat.

The Top-10% Chasers aren't interested in levelling the field—they just want VIP access to the one already tilted. If your feminism stops at the C-suite and skips the single mom at the checkout counter, you're not liberating women—you're just networking.

4. The Realists

Quiet. Competent. Tired as hell.

These are the women who actually keep the damn world turning.

They're not here to dunk on men or cosplay as girlbosses. They're raising families, leaving toxic jobs, surviving assault, navigating divorce, starting businesses, demanding justice, and still showing up to work with coffee and a little mascara smudged from crying in the car.

They don't scream "kill all men." They know better. They've seen good ones and bad ones. And they've learned not to generalize based on chromosomes but on *character.*

They're not trying to flip tables—they're just trying to get a damn seat. But you wouldn't know it from the feminist PR machine that prioritizes aesthetics over action. These women aren't loud enough to trend, but they're real enough to matter. And they're fed up with a movement that tells them they're not feminist enough unless they're angry, bitter, or terminally online.

If anyone deserves backup, it's them. But the movement left them behind. So maybe—just maybe—they should start turning to someone else.

Like... men.

Because here's the plot twist: some men are actually listening. Helping. Adapting. And the women worth fighting for? They know the difference between an ally and an adversary.

So if modern feminism wants to survive, it better decide:

Does it want followers?

Or does it want partners?

Because real change doesn't come from yelling at each other across gender lines. It comes from building bridges—and walking across them together.

The Case for Male Allies: Time to Hand Over the Blueprint

Here's a revolutionary idea that shouldn't feel revolutionary at all: what if women let men help? Not in the way of performative speeches and borrowed outrage, where a man loudly proclaims himself a feminist while angling for praise—or worse, a date—but in a way that acknowledges the quiet, real ones. The men who don't lead with hashtags, who've been listening more than talking, who feel the sting of being lumped in with predators but also understand where the rage comes from.

These aren't saviours in shining armour. They're not looking to command the movement. What they want—what women need—is for them to show up as they are: flawed, aware, and consistent. No applause necessary. No participation trophies. Just space to contribute meaningfully without needing to dominate the room.

The tired idea that men don't care about women's issues is lazy at best, dishonest at worst. The truth is, good men have been fighting quietly and thanklessly for a long time. They're the judges throwing the book at abusers, the teachers mentoring boys who might otherwise become statistics, the cops handling domestic calls with compassion instead of brute force, the dads raising daughters to speak up and sons to know when it's not their turn to speak.

You don't see them trending because "good judgment" and "ethical behaviour" don't go viral. But that doesn't mean their work isn't happening—or that it isn't vital. If anything, the fact that these efforts are invisible speaks volumes about how warped our metrics of value have become.

We keep talking about dismantling systems. But many of those systems—laws, hierarchies, boardroom cultures, and legislative frameworks—were designed by men in the first place. That doesn't mean men are uniquely suited to lead the fix, but it does mean they understand the faulty wiring better than most. If you inherit a crumbling mansion, would you rather bulldoze it with no plan or bring in someone who knows where the beams are cracked and the pipes are leaking?

Let's be honest: we're not short on brilliant women ready to rebuild the damn house from scratch. But when both genders understand the architecture, when there are engineers on both sides of the blueprint, the house gets renovated faster, safer, and smarter. This isn't about giving men back the pen. It's about letting them help draft the edits.

Emotionally intelligent men—those who've done the inner work and have no need to centre themselves—can bring something valuable to high-stakes, emotionally charged spaces: clarity without ego. These men don't deflect. They don't get defensive. And when they call out other men, they do it without performative outrage, because they understand that true allyship is done quietly, consistently, and without seeking attention.

A male ally is not a knight with a saviour complex. He's a sparring partner. He sharpens your instincts, watches your blind spots, and blocks incoming shots. His strength isn't in volume, but in discipline. His presence isn't to dominate—it's to stabilize.

The biggest misconception is that letting men in means letting them take over. No. It means letting them take responsibility without needing to lead. It means acknowledging women aren't fighting men; they're fighting a disease—entitlement, abuse, injustice, and silence. And men who are emotionally, socially, and ethically healthy? They can be the immune system that fights back.

They don't need to speak for women. They need to speak *with* them. They don't need to tear down patriarchy by themselves. But they sure as hell can help loosen the screws, carry some beams, and maybe—just maybe—start raising sons who won't need entire movements built to clean up their mess.

Progress doesn't mean locking the door behind men once they get in. It means drafting new blueprints and asking the right people to help build what's next. Some men are already on the construction site. It might be time women handed them the plans.

Redefining the Goal

Let's be clear: this isn't about trading high heels for hard hats just to prove women can. It's not about squeezing women into male-shaped moulds or pushing them up corporate ladders they had no hand in building. And it's certainly not about encouraging women to outwork, outdrink, or out-burnout the boys to earn a seat at a table that was never designed with them in mind.

That's not liberation—it's assimilation. And frankly, it's a trap. One that leaves too many women burned out, boxed in, and still feeling like outsiders wearing suits tailored for someone else's success story.

Real Empowerment Is Not a Costume Change

True empowerment isn't about showing the world that women can do what men do. It's about creating the conditions where women can do what they do best—on their own terms, in their own rhythms—and then supporting that with capital, credibility, and community.

We need to stop treating traditionally "feminine" skills and pursuits like quaint hobbies and start recognizing them for what they are: real work, real innovation, and real business. Men have been monetizing their hobbies for centuries—fishing, fantasy leagues, entire podcast empires about nothing in particular—and no one questions their legitimacy. But when a woman turns her talent for baking, crafting, caregiving, or organizing into a business, suddenly it's "cute," "small," or "just a side hustle."

Never mind that many of these women are more skilled, more disciplined, and more emotionally intelligent than half the tech bros lighting up your

LinkedIn feed. The issue isn't ambition—it's perception. And it's time that changed.

The System Wasn't Built With Women in Mind—But It Can Be Rebuilt With Them

Here's the part that makes people squirm: the economy, the tax code, the corporate world—almost every pillar of public life—was built by and for men, at a time when women were legally and socially excluded. That's not an opinion. That's history.

So when women step into these systems and find they don't quite fit, the problem isn't their competence. It's the rulebook. It was written without them in the room. The good news? Rules can be rewritten—and who better to do that than the ones who helped draft the originals?

This isn't about replacing men. It's about partnering with them to redesign the game so it's fairer, fuller, and more future-proof. Everyone deserves to play full court, not just half.

From Revenge to Recalibration

This movement is not about revenge. It's about

recalibration. It's not "make men pay" to even the score—it's "let's make sure no one has to pay like that again." Justice isn't about villains. It's about vision.

And that vision looks like women turning their passions into scalable businesses, with serious funding behind them. It looks like female artists and storytellers shaping culture, not just responding to it. It looks like motherhood being seen not just as a sacrifice, but as a masterclass in leadership, time management, negotiation, and emotional intelligence. It looks like men using their privilege not to take the mic, but to turn up the volume on voices that haven't been heard.

Rewrite the Blueprint—Together

This is the real revolution—not forcing women to fit into outdated spaces, but co-creating better ones. Not scrambling up broken ladders, but pouring solid floors that hold everyone up. When women are free to pursue what they love and master it without compromise, society doesn't fracture—it flourishes.

Profit follows passion. Power follows purpose. And progress? It always follows partnership.

What Needs to Change: A Cultural Detox for a Broken Blueprint

Let's cut the performance art. Society is not a hashtag, and no, slogans don't fix systemic rot. "Men are trash" won't compost into better men. Hypersexuality doesn't mend broken spirits. And no, pain should not be the entrance fee for credibility.

If we want to create a world where women thrive, not just survive, we need to stop glorifying the grind and start engineering the exit. The hustle, the trauma worship, the aestheticized suffering—it's all a scam. What women need is less martyrdom, more blueprints.

1. Raise Girls Beyond the Trauma Narrative

Can we stop prepping girls for a lifetime of dodging bullets before they even hit puberty? Childhood shouldn't feel like boot camp for survival. Every "Don't wear that," "Don't go there," "Don't make him angry" plants the idea that girlhood is an impending crime scene.

Let's change the script.

Girls are not future cautionary tales. They are not "strong because they suffered." They are powerful because they exist with brains, instincts, and talents that don't need trauma to be validated.

Instead of trauma response training, let's teach self-trust. Let's raise curious minds, not obedient bodies. Teach them their worth *before* someone tries to negotiate it down to trauma porn.

We don't need more survivors. We need more builders, coders, creators, leaders—unapologetically whole.

2. Redesign Systems—Not Just Assign Women to the Dysfunction

You can't put a woman in a broken system and call it progress. That's not equity. That's camouflage.

We keep handing women a seat at the table, then forgetting to mention the table's on fire. Burnout, workplace harassment, unrealistic expectations—and we call it "opportunity."

No thanks.

We need systems that don't just include women but are *informed* by them. Workplaces where caregiving is assumed, not excused. Leadership that rewards empathy and efficiency, not how long you can fake productivity behind a desk. Boards that are built for collaboration, not gladiator games.

You want real change? Stop painting the patriarchy pink. Start redesigning the architecture.

3. Ditch the Clickbait Feminism

"Men are trash."

"Sleep your way to healing."

"Burn it all down."

This isn't empowerment—it's bumper sticker nihilism with a side of Instagram filters. It sells rage instead of reform and confuses viral content with virtue.

Complex problems require nuance. Hard conversations. Accountability on all sides. And yes, that means acknowledging that some of what's sold as "feminism" today is just repackaged vengeance.

Healing doesn't come from hating half the population. You can critique masculinity without crucifying men. You can demand better without pretending women are flawless saints floating above the fray.

If women want to be taken seriously, they need to act like grown-ups, not meme accounts.

4. Stop Selling Chaos as Liberation

Let's not confuse freedom with frenzy.

We've created this weird double standard where self-destruction is called "empowerment" as long as it's wearing eyeliner and tweeting about astrology. But here's the deal: whether it's a man or a woman spiralling through meaningless sex, binge culture, or emotional detachment, it's not strength. It's avoidance in costume.

If a man did it, we'd stage an intervention. But when a woman does it? We hand her a brand deal and call it "owning her narrative."

Liberation isn't about how much chaos you can endure. It's about how much clarity you can create. It's not about how many people you can collect, discard, or ghost. It's about learning to sit with your pain, process it, and *build something better.*

Freedom without direction is just another kind of prison.

5. Start with Honesty. Then Add Humility.

We don't need more empowerment merch or half-baked TikTok mantras. We need a cultural detox.

That starts with truth. Women being honest about what's broken and what's performative. Men stepping up—not as heroes, but as reliable partners. Both sides putting down the ego and picking up the blueprints.

Change doesn't come from dominance. It comes from co-creation. Mutual reinforcement. Shared sacrifice. Strategic unity.

This is not about becoming invincible. It's about becoming *interdependent*—building something so stable and honest that no single storm can collapse it.

We're not rivals. We're co-authors.

The future won't be written in hashtags. It won't be won on Twitter threads or performance outrage. It'll be built in boardrooms, classrooms, homes, and studios—by people who show up with humility, direction, and the guts to rewrite the blueprint.

Everything else?

Just noise.

And we've got better things to build than noise.

The Rebuild: Not Revenge, But Recalibration

Let's get one thing straight: liberation is *not* a costume change. Women weren't put on this planet to become carbon copies of men just to validate their worth. Women weren't meant to survive the system's grind—they were meant to *reshape* it. Yet, for too long, the narrative shoved at them has been assimilation: "Succeed like a man. Hustle like a man. Climb like a man. Think like a man." Spoiler alert—this isn't freedom. It's a squeeze into a mould someone else designed, then painted pink and called it empowerment.

True liberation isn't mimicry. It's creation. It's a bold, collective construction of something new—something built *together.*

Women Don't Need to Win a War. They Need to Design Peace.

Liberation begins with raising girls who know their value without having to bleed for it. Girls who aren't groomed to be survivors of trauma but nurtured to be architects of purpose. Because here's the truth: potential doesn't spring from pain; it blooms from clarity, drive, and intention.

It means tearing up the flawed blueprints and rewriting the damn systems. Systems that reward empathy, creativity, and partnership, not outdated dominance and hierarchy. It means discarding the clickbait culture of rage and hashtag resistance, because revolutions that matter don't trend—they *persist.*

They happen in quiet, stubborn ways:

A father teaching his daughter to walk through life with confidence, not fear.

A male colleague speaking up for his female peer, not as a knight in shining armour, but as an equal.

A woman choosing clarity over chaos, vision over vengeance, *purpose* over performance.

Men Are Not the Enemy. They're the Missing Link.

Here's a radical idea: let men in. Not as the generals of this new battle, but as allies in the build. After all, they crafted many of the systems women want to dismantle—so why not bring them in to help rebuild? Not from a place of guilt or shame, but from grace and strategic partnership.

When good men show up—not to rescue or dominate but to reinforce—they speed up progress. They don't need to save anyone, just stand beside women, wielding power, policy, and presence as tools of transformation.

This Is a Partnership, Not a Performance

Imagine raising women who unapologetically love their gifts and know how to monetize them without hand-wringing. Imagine raising men who admire strength without feeling the need to crush it. Imagine a culture where equality isn't a battleground, but a blueprint.

This isn't about settling old scores or erasing masculinity. It's about inviting it to evolve, mature, collaborate, and build.

Because here's the bottom line: humanity only wins when both men and women win. Anything less? It's just marketing noise—pretty packaging for the same old story.

And frankly, we've got better stories to write.

Universal Laws, Not Identity Games

The Myth of Empowerment Through Fragmentation

Let's start with a simple, boring demographic fact: women outnumber men after age 15. This should be an earth-shattering statistic if we believed in strength in numbers. Mathematically, women should be unstoppable. Strategically, women should run the damn planet. But instead, they've managed to turn majority power into minority performance—because every woman wants her own private liberation party.

Women have taken the idea of collective empowerment and ripped it to pieces like a sale rack at Target. Instead of uniting, women specialize. Women fracture. Women splinter into acronyms and hashtags like niche indie bands, each with a cult following, no mainstream traction, and a GoFundMe that goes nowhere. Black feminism. Trans-inclusive feminism. TERFs. SWERFs. Rich feminism. Eco-feminism. Intersectional feminism with gluten-free labelling. Pick your poison—or make your own.

But here's the kicker: a thousand micro-movements don't add up to a revolution. They just add up to a noisy, infighting mess where every group is more concerned with being "seen" than being *effective*. If activism were a group project, feminism would be the one where everyone insists on doing their own slide, because no one likes working with *that* girl.

Oppression Olympics: The Gold Medal of Nowhere

Let's not forget the trauma badge economy, where victimhood has become its own currency. The more specific and painful your struggle, the more moral capital you can claim. It's not enough to say you're oppressed; you must be oppressed *uniquely*. Bonus points if your pain is misunderstood by at least four other subgroups. This has led to a strange performance art where everyone wants to win the Oppression Olympics, but no one wants to fix the stadium at the brink of collapse.

Suddenly, women are not fighting patriarchy. They're fighting each other to prove whose struggle is more aesthetically devastating. God forbid you're just a regular working-class woman with no curated trauma—*boring!* Your pain doesn't get a podcast or a panel. In this ecosystem, if your oppression can't be neatly branded or monetized, you might as well be invisible.

Branding Over Building

Empowerment used to mean structural change. Now it means brand identity. "Empowered" women are influencers with ring lights and trauma merch, not policy-makers or community organizers. Everyone's starting a "movement," which is often just a rebranded blog post with a new logo and some merch.

Meanwhile, basic needs are still unmet. Women are still dying in childbirth. Still earning less. Still being assaulted and dismissed. But go off, queen—launch that Kickstarter for a feminist wine label. We'll toast to equality once the apocalypse is over.

The Tyranny of Specificity

Here's the hard truth: you can't scale specificity. Not in politics. Not in policy. Not in power. If your liberation plan can't be replicated outside of your zip code, your skin tone, or your dating preference, it's not a movement, it's a memoir.

Yes, different women face different struggles. But when you make every single issue an island, you lose the power of unity. Fragmentation might make you feel special, but it won't make you safe. A united movement builds schools, clinics, and laws. A divided one builds Twitter threads and resentment.

Revenge of the Universal

Imagine for one moment if women—*all* women—fought for access to education, affordable healthcare, and violence prevention with the same intensity they fight for representation in Vogue. We'd have global change within a decade. But we don't. Because that doesn't get likes, book deals, or TED talks.

Universal goals aren't sexy. They're not glamorous. But they work. They lift entire generations. They're the reason you even have the luxury to argue about the rest.

Get Over Yourself, Join the Fight

This is not a call to erase identity—it's a call to outgrow it as a limitation. We can celebrate our differences without making them the hill every battle has to die on. Empowerment isn't a Pinterest board of affirmations. It's showing up—even when it's not about you.

So yes, keep your hyphens and hashtags. But build something bigger than your bio. Because until women stop slicing themselves into smaller, trendier pieces, the patriarchy will always win by default.

Stop Chasing Special — Start Choosing Strategic

Modern feminism has a branding issue—and not the cute kind with fonts and colours, but the kind that sinks ships. Somewhere along the line, the movement decided that being *strategic* was boring, and being *special* was everything. The result? A political philosophy that looks less like a coalition and more like a talent show—except everyone's trying to out-trauma each other instead of even making up a mediocre performance.

It's a race to be *the exception*, not the solution. The only thing more powerful than a woman these days is a woman with a *niche struggle*. "I'm not just fighting patriarchy," she says, "I'm doing it as a left-handed, vegan, neurodivergent descendant of colonial trauma with a startup." Everyone wants to be the main character. And movements full of main characters? They go nowhere fast—usually in high heels and holding protest signs with glitter fonts.

No One Builds an Army Out of Solo Acts

You can't build a movement on a million one-woman shows. It's like trying to fight a war with interpretive dancers instead of soldiers. Looks cool for five seconds; accomplishes nothing.

The problem is simple: collective power doesn't come from uniqueness, it comes from shared objectives. But shared objectives require compromise, patience, and worst of all, not being the centre of attention. Which is basically kryptonite to the modern activist industrial complex.

Everyone wants their fight to be the most urgent, the most funded, the most promoted. The idea of combining forces, setting priorities, and building coalitions? That's considered selling out—unless it comes with a Netflix documentary.

From Mars to Maternity Wards

Let's talk about priorities, shall we? Because right now, we've got thinkpieces about how we need more women in venture capital, more women in crypto, more women in STEM fields building blockchain startups for pet DNA. That's nice and all, but how about more women who don't bleed to death in childbirth? Or more girls who get to finish high school before being sold off into marriage? Or working moms who aren't one flat tire away from homelessness?

Instead of chasing prestige projects that benefit 0.01% of women (and usually already-rich ones), how about fixing the rusted-out floorboards of basic survival? But no, apparently that's not "aspirational" enough for keynote speeches and feminist TEDx salons with $19 water bottles.

It's a branding issue. Helping poor women get clean water won't trend like "women in aerospace." Fighting for fair labour laws in textile factories isn't sexy like "female founders in AI." But here's the kicker: basic victories scale. Prestige victories don't.

Strategic > Symbolic

Symbolic wins look good. Strategic wins *work*. That's the difference.

You can get 50 more women into Parliament tomorrow, but if they're ineffective, spineless, or just replicating male mediocrity in new suits, it's a net zero. You can scream about "representation" all day, but if nothing changes on the ground, it's just optics. Women don't need to see themselves in power—they need power to work in their lives.

So what's the solution? Simple. Start thinking like generals, not influencers. Stop choosing battles that look good in press releases and start picking fights that *actually matter*. Education. Health care. Legal protections. Employment rights. Reproductive support (real support, not just hashtags).

Win something real. Then win something bigger.

Less Clout, More Cohesion

If this movement wants to survive the next generation, it needs to grow up. No more stunt activism. No more abstract art exhibitions masquerading as resistance. No more confusing visibility with victory.

Want to be special? Get a loyal boyfriend. Want to be effective? Pick battles that build power for millions, not just prestige for you.

Let the influencers chase their blue checkmarks. Real strategists build legacies.

Universal Priorities Over Elite Preferences

Let's skip the polite introductions: the top 10% of women already live like the top 10% of men. They have Pilates memberships, HR departments, and lawyers on retainer. Their struggles are real, but they're not relatable. And if a movement builds its agenda around their anxieties, it's not a movement. It's a luxury brand.

You don't make progress by throwing gala fundraisers for problems the average woman can't pronounce. You make progress by fixing what's broken at scale: the infrastructure of dignity, safety, and survival that most women live without. Until we stop confusing elite preferences with universal needs, this entire gender-wide campaign is going to keep looking like a TED Talk that nobody in a rural town can afford to attend.

Domestic Abuse: Not Just a Hashtag for Awareness Month

Let's start with the obvious. If a woman's access to safety depends on her zip code, her bank balance, or whether she knows how to code-switch at a shelter, the system is broken.

Domestic abuse support isn't supposed to be artisanal. It doesn't need a rebrand. It needs funding, training, accessibility, and teeth. The average woman doesn't need a campaign. She needs a working hotline and a place to go where she won't be told, "Sorry, we're full unless you have kids or bruises."

Stop designing trauma response systems that look good on annual reports and start building ones that work in real life.

Maternity Protections: Not a Favour—A Functioning Policy

Maternity is still treated like a productivity error by most companies and a personal decision that the government barely tolerates. The message is clear: "Thanks for populating the workforce. Now try not to bleed on the company timecard."

Pregnancy isn't rare. It's not radical. It's the reason we exist. And yet maternity protections—leave, medical care, reentry support—are either nonexistent, predatory, or laughably short in most parts of the world. You want to empower women? Start by making sure giving birth doesn't derail their income, destroy their career, or bankrupt their household.

Healthcare: All of It. Everywhere.

Health care should be non-negotiable, especially when it comes to reproductive and mental health—but here we are, still debating it like it's a luxury add-on. And before someone says "access exists," let's be clear: access isn't the same as affordability, usability, or not having to Google your symptoms at 3 am because you're afraid of the bill.

Reproductive rights don't stop at abortion, and mental health support isn't a podcast ad for CBD gummies. Women need real doctors, real policies, and real support—not digital "awareness" campaigns that go viral and vanish.

Employment Laws: Still Built for Men With Wives at Home

Most employment laws still operate on the assumption that the "ideal worker" is a man with a stay-at-home partner who keeps his shirts ironed and the kids alive. Any deviation from that—say, a single mother or a pregnant woman—is considered a logistical problem.

If the first thing that crumbles when a woman gets pregnant is her job security, that's not a "female issue." That's a structural design flaw in the economy. Fix it.

Flexible hours. Paid leave. No more "motherhood penalty" in hiring. And definitely no more asking women in job interviews if they "plan to start a family anytime soon"—unless you're also asking men if they plan to ghost their kids.

Sanitary Products: Dignity, Not a Designer Item

If we lived in a rational world, basic menstrual hygiene would be treated like toilet paper: boring, everywhere, and free. Instead, it's still taxed, considered a taboo by some, and treated like a specialty product—because apparently, having a uterus is a subscription-based inconvenience.

This isn't edgy policy. It's basic human dignity. And yet the conversation still gets sidelined like it's some fringe concern. Meanwhile, millions of girls drop out of school or skip work every month because they literally can't afford to bleed.

Start at the Bottom. That's Where the Base Is.

Movements don't fail because they don't have elite buy-in. They fail because they forget the base. You don't build a revolution by starting with keynote speakers and working your way down to sanitation. You build it from the bottom up.

Fix what's universal first: health, safety, dignity. Then you can talk about board seats and biotech equity without sounding like you're curating feminism for LinkedIn.

And no, the basics aren't "lesser" goals. They're the goals that *actually scale*. Universal wins are sticky. They build trust, legitimacy, and momentum. Every girl who gets a free education becomes a potential voter, leader, or innovator. Every mother who doesn't get fired for giving birth is a walking policy endorsement. That's how you build a durable legacy, not a boutique ideology.

The Top's Already Fine. Build for the Base.

If feminism is going to evolve into something more than a PR campaign for wealthy women with PR managers and personal stylists, it has to stop chasing boutique reforms and start laying bricks where the pavement ends.

Power comes from numbers. But real numbers live in reality, not in conference rooms, not in curated panels, and definitely not in expensive panel discussions about "breaking the glass ceiling" while most women are still sweeping the floor.

Fix the basics. Then we'll talk about Mars.

Competence Over Optics in Leadership

Let's get one thing straight: representation without competence is just decoration. It might look nice in press releases and perform well on Twitter, but when the curtain lifts and the leadership collapses under basic scrutiny, it's not just a personal failure—it becomes a collective indictment.

This is the double-bind. When a man fails in office, he's just a bad leader. When a woman fails, she's a case study in why women shouldn't lead. It's unfair, but it's also reality. So the solution isn't to whine about the unfairness; it's to choose leaders who can survive the weight of scrutiny, perform under pressure, and deliver results. Until failure is a luxury that women can afford without dragging down their entire gender, competence isn't optional—it's the floor.

The Symbolic Trap: The Girlboss Placeholder

There's a special breed of appointment that happens when institutions want to look progressive but still function exactly the same: the symbolic hire. You've seen it. The woman tapped to lead a collapsing department, a dying company, or a scandal-ridden institution—not because she's the best option, but because she's a "fresh face" with optics appeal. In short: a scapegoat in lipstick.

She's handed a grenade with the pin half-pulled, and when the thing goes off, the story writes itself: "See? We tried diversity, and it didn't work." Meanwhile, men have been blowing up institutions for centuries without their gender being questioned.

If you wouldn't hire a man with no track record to lead a complex system, don't hire a woman just to check a demographic box. That's not progress. That's sabotage with better lighting.

Stop the 'First Woman to...' Obsession

Celebrating "firsts" is great—until it becomes the entire metric. Being the first woman to do something is not the same as being the right person to do it. At some point, we have to stop acting like gender is a credential. It isn't. It's a context. It adds insight. It adds experience. But if it's the only selling point? That's a red flag.

Every time someone says, "She's making history!" ask a better question: *Is she making progress?*

What Competence Actually Looks Like

Competence doesn't trend on social media. It doesn't wear slogan T-shirts or hold press conferences about empowerment. It reads the policy brief, runs the numbers, shows up on time, and gets the job done. It's unsexy. It's thankless. And it's what separates the leaders who create real change from those who just pose in front of a billboard.

Want to fix things? Appoint women who understand the mission, not just the optics. Hire the candidate who can survive the battlefield, not just the panel discussion.

No More Sacrificial Lambs

If we're serious about equality, we need to stop treating leadership as a marketing campaign and start treating it like a high-stakes responsibility. That means no more sacrificial lambs with perfect Instagram feeds and zero relevant experience. It means saying no to vanity appointments and yes to proven strategists—even if they don't fit the glossy mould.

Here's a radical thought: Maybe the most empowering thing we can do is stop pretending every woman in power is automatically good for women.

Some are incompetent. Some are corrupt. Some are simply not up to the job. And that's okay, *as long as we're allowed to say it out loud without being accused of misogyny.*

Equality Means Earning It—And Owning It

The real test of equality? When women can be fired for sucking at their jobs without it being a civil rights crisis. That's when women would've made it. Until then, we need to be ruthless about one thing: skill over symbolism. Not because women need to be perfect, but because we're still living in a world where they can't afford not to be.

Women don't need more icons. They need more professionals.

Women don't need symbolic wins. They need strategic ones.

And Women definitely don't need another "girlboss" at the helm of a slow-moving disaster, only to have her gender retroactively blamed for the collapse.

Hire better. Expect more. Lead with competence. Then—and only then—will the optics take care of themselves.

Lead From the Front, Not From a Hashtag

There's a certain type of modern "leader" who never seems to break a sweat. Their revolution comes with curated lighting, a matching hoodie, and a hashtag. They're brave from the safety of their home office. Bold in the comments section. Fierce in a pre-recorded TED Talk with three rounds of edits and a makeup team. But when the actual fight shows up—when there's a risk to reputation, livelihood, or personal comfort? Crickets. Or worse, a statement.

Let's be blunt: you don't get to call yourself a leader if you're allergic to consequences.

Influence Isn't Leadership

The internet has created a whole generation of illusionists: people who've confused visibility with value. They think viral posts are strategy, and engagement stats are proof of courage. But leadership isn't a Wi-Fi signal. You can't beam it in. You have to show up. On the ground. In the mess. In the chaos. Not to film it—but to fix it.

If your biggest risk is a temporary dip in followers, you're not a leader—you're a lifestyle brand.

The Myth of the Painless Movement

Somewhere along the way, the word "activist" lost its spine. It became a job title for people whose main weapon is Canva templates and whose biggest war wound is being ratioed on Twitter. Real activism costs something. Reputation. Money. Safety. Time. If it doesn't hurt, even a little, it's probably just marketing.

Movements aren't built by people who dip in for applause and dip out at the first sign of backlash. They're built by those who take the first hit and stay for the clean-up.

Command Without Risk Is Cowardice

There's no shortage of people who want to call the shots from a safe distance. The "leadership" class has become obsessed with abstraction—issuing bold directives from climate-controlled rooms while leaving the grunt work to volunteers, interns, or the eternally expendable "grassroots."

But if you're not in the trenches with the people you claim to represent, you don't represent them. You're just cosplaying leadership with none of the wear and tear.

You don't get to lead from the back of the line. You don't get to outsource the risk and hoard the credit. That's not leadership—it's cowardice in a power suit.

Real Leaders Eat Last—And Bleed First

True leadership isn't about aesthetics or slogans. It's about being the first into the fire and the last to leave the rubble. It's about staying when the press leaves, when the budget dries up, when it's no longer popular or convenient or trending.

You go first. You stay the longest. You lose sleep. You lose comfort. Sometimes, you lose everything. That's the price.

And it's worth it—because real movements don't need figureheads. They need *anchors*.

Burn the Hashtag, Bring the Hammer

We don't need more brand ambassadors for justice. We don't need more speeches about "raising awareness" while the house burns down behind them. We need people who *move*, who *build*, who *sacrifice*. The ones who don't need a camera to show up. The ones who would do it even if no one ever clapped.

Because here's the uncomfortable truth: Hashtags don't change systems. People do. But only when they stop waiting to be seen and start being willing to bleed.

So, if you're not ready to sweat, lose, or bleed for the cause, step aside. The front line isn't for influencers.

The Power of Small Wins

Want to know the fastest way to kill a movement? Swing for the moon, miss spectacularly, and then blame the system while your audience quietly unsubscribes from caring. That's how you turn once-loyal supporters into skeptics. Because here's the thing: people don't rally around vibes—they rally around results.

We've spent too long treating activism like a pitch deck for venture capital. "Ten women in space! A billionaire girlboss with a yacht! Look, she's leaning in!" Meanwhile, half the world's women can't afford sanitary pads, and the other half are getting gaslit out of maternity leave. We've confused aspiration with strategy.

Education Over Elevation

Putting ten more women into Fortune 500 boardrooms doesn't change much, not for the 99% of women who will never set foot in one. But give a girl in a rural village access to school? You've just rewritten her entire bloodline. You've reduced child marriage, increased economic output, improved health outcomes, and planted the seeds for generational change. All for less than what it costs to sponsor a single corporate diversity workshop that teaches everyone to say "Latinx" and feel accomplished.

That's power. Measurable. Repeatable. Revolutionary.

Not performative. Not prestige-driven. Just solid, real-world returns.

Win Small, Win Early, Win Loud

You want support? Show wins. Small wins. Visible wins. Repeatable wins. You don't start a war by capturing the capital—you start by taking the outposts, building momentum, and making the enemy bleed belief. If people don't believe change is possible, they don't fight for it. But give them a few victories, and they'll fight like hell.

A mother who survives childbirth because of better prenatal care is a win.

A girl who finishes high school because of free sanitary products is a win.

A single mom who doesn't lose her job for giving birth is a win.

These aren't symbolic. They're foundational. Every one of them chips away at systems of inequality while building public trust in reform.

The Faith Economy of Change

Movements run on faith. If people believe you're winning, they'll invest. Time, money, and energy. But when your biggest milestone is another influencer panel discussing "the female gaze in cryptocurrency," people start wondering if they're being played.

Progress doesn't have to be sexy. It just has to work.

Less Hype, More Proof

Social change isn't a TED Talk—it's a ledger. What changed? For who? How many? Can we do it again? If you can't answer those, you're not running a movement. You're running a speaking tour. The future isn't won by dreamers—it's won by doers. And the doers start small, win fast, and use that momentum to bulldoze the next wall.

So, stop trying to go viral and start trying to go *visible*. Build a better school. Fund a clinic. Change a policy. Get a law passed. Then repeat. That's how revolutions are born—not in tweets, but in towns.

Because if you want to shake the world, you don't start with a press release.

You start with a girl reading her first book.

Play the Long Game: Legacy Over Ego

You don't build a cathedral in a weekend. You lay bricks, one at a time, knowing damn well you'll be dead before the stained glass even shows up. That's legacy. That's maturity. And frankly, that's the kind of thinking missing from most modern activism.

We've turned change into a personal brand—microwaved outrage, instant gratification, and a thirst for moral credit that expires faster than a tweet. Everyone wants to be the face of the movement, no one wants to be the skeleton under the foundation.

Here's the uncomfortable truth: this generation probably won't see the promised land.

And that's not a failure—that's how real progress works.

Ego Wants a Crown—Legacy Builds a Ladder

Every few months, there's a new saviour with a slogan. A new viral push promising *this* will be the revolution that finally "fixes everything." Spoiler: it won't. Because the hard stuff—the *real* stuff—can't be solved in one hashtag cycle or by electing one more "historic first."

What's needed is compound interest in progress—small, sustained improvements that future generations can build on. Think less messiah, more mason.

Start policies now so your granddaughters aren't fighting the same battles.

Build schools you'll never attend.

Pass laws that benefit people you'll never meet.

It's not romantic. It's not flashy. It's just how every lasting civilization, reform, or rights movement has ever worked.

The Relay, Not the Race

Everyone wants to break the tape. No one wants to run the middle stretch—the thankless, exhausting part with no fanfare. But that's where legacies are made. That's where history gets carried forward.

It's not about being the hero—it's about not dropping the baton.

The suffragettes didn't march, so you could hold up a sign for Instagram. They bled, went to prison, starved, and got mocked for decades. And they never got to vote themselves. They passed it forward.

So what are *you* passing forward?

The Thousand Miles Myth

Trying to sprint a thousand-mile journey in one go isn't ambition—it's delusion. Burnout disguised as virtue. You don't need to move the mountain. Just chip off your piece. Do it well. Do it honestly. And make it easier for the next handoff.

Let someone else plant the flag.

You do the landscaping.

Your daughters will pave the road.

Your granddaughters will build the sign that says: *this way forward.*

Your great-granddaughters will have a smooth ride to the promised land.

Because if every generation tries to be the finale, there won't be a next act.

The Real Measure

Want to know if your movement is working? Look at your grandkids.

If they don't know what you fought for—because they didn't *have* to—then you won.

That's the goal.

No statue. No award. Just a generation that doesn't have to fight the same war you did. Not because it disappeared, but because you handled your stretch of the road so well, they could finally cruise instead of hike.

That's the long game.

And it's the only one worth playing.

Redefining What Women's Issues Actually Are

If you asked most media outlets or college panels to list "women's issues," they'd rattle off the same headline hitters: abortion access, more women in boardrooms, more women in office, and equal pay. And sure, those matter—but the framing is broken. Not wrong. Just wildly incomplete.

Because here's a cold truth: you can't fight for equality on a marble floor when half the world's women are still trying to get access to basic human needs.

The Pyramid Problem

We've built our advocacy upside down. Like a pyramid balanced on its tip—top-heavy with elite preferences, feather-light at the base. We've let the loudest voices define the battlefield, and shocker: those voices usually have Ivy League degrees, dual incomes, and a podcast.

Meanwhile, women without clean water, prenatal care, or a place to escape their abusers are somehow expected to cheer for another symbolic glass ceiling shatter. You want applause? Try handing them a working toilet first.

The Boring Stuff That Saves Lives

Here's what *should* be on the priority list:

- Sanitary products: Not diamond-encrusted period panties—basic pads. Available, free, and reliable. Because managing menstruation shouldn't be an act of logistical genius.
- Prenatal and postpartum care: You can't scream "every life matters" while women die in labour for lack of transport or funding. Pregnancy shouldn't be a poverty sentence or a death risk.
- Safe spaces for abuse survivors: Not Instagram support groups—actual shelters. Beds. Lawyers. Doors that lock.
- Affordable childcare: If a woman has to choose between working and feeding her kids, we don't need more empowerment speeches. We need infrastructure.
- Mental health care tailored to women: Hormones aren't excuses—they're real, cyclical, and ignored. Male-centred diagnostics don't cut it when you're breaking down during ovulation, and no one believes you.

These aren't sexy topics. They don't trend. They don't sell merch.

But they keep people alive.

Until Survival Is Universal, Thriving Is a Distraction

I'm not saying stop fighting for abortion rights or high-ranking promotions. But don't pretend you're winning just because one woman made it to the Senate in heels. That's a win for *her*, not necessarily for the rest.

Movements lose when they mistake milestones for mass change. And they *die* when they trade survival for symbolism.

You want to know what a feminist victory looks like?

A pregnant woman in a low-income neighbourhood sees a doctor *before* labour.

An abused wife escapes *without* having to leave her kids behind.

That's the real frontline.

So let's stop confusing who gets the microphone with who needs the megaphone.

Until every woman has a chance to thrive, feminists have no business obsessing over who gets to break the glass ceiling.

This Is About Collective Survival, Not Personal Branding

Being a woman isn't an aesthetic. It's not a marketing angle or a curated feed theme. It's not some Instagram filter with a "Boss Babe" quote slapped on top. It's a lived experience—one shaped by geography, income, religion, biology, and culture. And yet, somehow, activism has been hijacked by influencers who think a hashtag and a t-shirt equal revolution.

Spoiler alert: if your feminism can't survive outside of a borrowed Wi-Fi range, it's not a movement. It's a brand campaign.

You're Not a Movement, You're a Mood Board

Too much modern advocacy looks like this: a trending issue, a new merch drop, a photo in front of a protest sign (with the logo facing out), and a caption that sounds like ChatGPT trying to be woke.

But here's the problem: you can't TikTok your way out of systemic inequality. You can't put "activist" in your bio and call it a day. And you sure as hell can't build a political movement by treating oppression like a networking opportunity.

Real movements don't run on optics. They run on sacrifice, strategy, and unglamorous, backbreaking work. The kind that doesn't trend. The kind no one claps for.

If It Doesn't Scale, It Doesn't Matter

If your version of progress only applies to women who:

- Speak English fluently
- Have access to reliable electricity
- Live in liberal democracies
- Are college-educated
- Know how to navigate bureaucracy

...then congrats: you've created a very exclusive club with a feminist logo on the door. Not a movement.

Meanwhile, the woman hauling water in 40-degree heat isn't worried about Lean In. She's worried about her kid dying of dysentery. The girl marrying at 13 doesn't need a TED Talk—she needs a legal system that protects her. The mother in a refugee camp doesn't need empowerment slogans. She needs food.

Build Systems, Not Selfies

Women don't need more viral moments. They need frameworks that *function*.

That means:

- Localized healthcare policies
- Community-led education initiatives

- Legal aid that reaches beyond capital cities
- Protection systems for domestic workers, not just tech CEOs
- Infrastructure that doesn't collapse after one PR cycle

You want change? Build boring things that last. Build without your name in lights. And when it works, let others take credit if it means the work continues.

The Real Litmus Test

Here's how you know if your activism is real:

Would you still do it if no one ever found out you did it?

Because if the answer is no, if your feminism disappears without a follow count, then it was never about survival. It was about self-promotion.

And women don't need more figureheads.

They need co-conspirators.

So let's stop mistaking clout for consequence.

Let's stop running clubs and start building coalitions.

Not everything has to be sexy. Just effective.

The NGO–Influencer Industrial Complex: Where Morality Meets Monetization

Let's talk about the shadow merger no one asked for but everyone pretends to love: the unholy alliance between non-governmental organizations (NGOs) and influencers. One was meant to save lives. The other was meant to sell lip gloss. Now they co-parent a monster built on donor dollars, Instagram filters, and the illusion of progress.

We used to look to NGOs for structural change—advocacy, service delivery, and actual work. Now? We get international development as curated content. Poverty with a sepia tone. Empowerment stories with brand deals attached. The cause hasn't changed. But the *packaging*? Immaculate.

Virtue as a Business Model

In theory, NGOs exist to help people. In practice, many exist to exist—to keep funding flowing, staff employed, and board members clapping at galas. And what better way to keep that cash rolling in than slapping a well-lit selfie of a "global changemaker" in front of a mud hut and calling it awareness?

Meanwhile, the actual women in the story? They become props. Silent, grateful, and above all, *non-complicated*. Tragedy sells, but only if it's the right aesthetic. Raw enough to evoke emotion, sanitized enough to not upset donors during brunch.

Influencers show up to the village in linen, take a few photos with barefoot children, and leave before the diarrhea kicks in. "Changing lives," they write in the caption. No one asks how. No one follows up.

Hashtag Humanitarianism

The NGO–influencer partnership thrives on one dirty little secret: donor fatigue is real. And what cures fatigue? A fresh face. A catchy hashtag. A viral moment. Enter the influencer.

- She's got 500k followers.
- She says "feminist" in five languages.
- She cries on camera once every three months.
- She posts her "difficult decision" to forgo first class for the mission trip.

Suddenly, she's the face of female empowerment in Sierra Leone. No language skills. No cultural understanding. But a killer Lightroom preset and a publicist who calls her "a bridge between worlds."

NGOs love it. Influencers love it. The algorithm loves it.

The only people not benefiting are the women it's supposedly for.

Change That Performs, Not Change That Persists

This industry is allergic to long timelines. It wants the dopamine hit of change, not the gruelling discomfort of actually building it. Schools are "opened" (read: photographed), projects are "launched" (read: tweeted), and results are "ongoing" (read: nobody checks back).

We don't measure success anymore—we measure *impressions*. Impact reports are now infographics. And success isn't whether the program worked; it's whether it got into *Forbes Women*.

The result? A feedback loop of meaningless visibility:

- NGOs compete for influencer attention.
- Influencers compete for NGO campaigns.
- The audience scrolls past, vaguely inspired but no better informed.

Who Gets Left Behind?

The same women are always left behind:

- The woman who doesn't speak English, so her story gets edited for clarity (read: whitewashed).
- The survivor who doesn't smile enough for the brand aesthetic.
- The girl who's too old, too dark, too poor, or too *real* to fit the empowerment narrative.

This complex doesn't elevate marginalized women. It markets them. And then discards them once they're no longer emotionally profitable.

Solutions? Or Just More Storylines?

What's the way out? Hint: it's not a new campaign. It's a reckoning.

- Kill the saviour narrative. Replace it with local leadership.
- Defund performative partnerships. Fund scalable infrastructure.
- Stop chasing visibility. Chase accountability.
- Audit results—not reach. And ask: who actually got helped?

Because a movement that needs a ring light to function is not a movement—it's content with a mission statement.

And if you're changing the world but still have time for a branded skincare tutorial in the same trip, maybe it's not the world you're saving.

Maybe it's just your *bank account*.

Burn the Costume, Build the Core

It's time we stop mistaking movement for progress and branding for belief. The modern feminist machine—hijacked by elite interests, flattened into hashtags, and pumped through NGO-influencer pipelines—has become a theatre of the absurd. Everyone's dressed for the revolution, but no one's building it.

We've substituted systemic change with symbolic gestures. Real power with curated empowerment. Strategy with spectacle. The result? A stage full of characters—girlboss CEOs, glamorized survivors, influencer "advocates"—all auditioning for applause while the majority of women still struggle to afford tampons or survive childbirth.

This chapter wasn't a call to cancel anyone. It was a call to unplug the amplifier and fix the wiring. Start with the unsexy stuff: enforcement, education, infrastructure, accountability. Build systems that don't need a face to function. Prioritize collective power over personal branding. Lead not to be seen, but to get shit done.

Because when the cameras go off and the algorithms shift, the work that matters will still be waiting.

And it won't care how many followers you have.

Competence Over Passion

Passion Is a Privilege — Competence Is Survival

The delusion of "do what you love" in a world that only pays for results

"Do what you love and you'll never work a day in your life," they say. But for most people, especially working-class women, doing what you love just means doing unpaid labour with a smile. Try telling the single mom working two jobs that she just needs to "find her passion," and she might stab you with her third-hand kitchen knife. Spoiler: it won't be out of passion.

The whole "follow your dreams" mantra sounds inspiring—until the rent is due. It's lifestyle advice dressed up as career guidance, sold by people who've never had to choose between groceries and gas. Passion is cute when your basic needs are covered. But if you're born without a safety net? Passion is a con. A marketing slogan disguised as life wisdom. Something you only hear from people whose dad paid for their "finding myself" year abroad in Lisbon while they "freelanced" in a café.

Let's say it plainly: passion is a luxury good. Like organic shampoo or unpaid internships. It's affordable only to those who can fail safely. For everyone else, it's a trapdoor hidden under a motivational quote.

Competence Doesn't Lie. Passion Does.

Passion is moody. One day you love photography, the next you hate dealing with clients and editing 400 wedding shots of a couple who met on Tinder while attending the same crypto conference abroad. Passion promises meaning; competence delivers money.

What no one puts on those Pinterest boards is the inconvenient truth: what you love doesn't always love you back. And it sure as hell doesn't owe you a living. You can adore painting watercolours of emotionally distant wolves, but unless those wolves are doing something NFT-worthy, no one's buying.

Competence, though? It doesn't care how you feel. It doesn't need your tears, your childhood dreams, or your spiritual alignment. It just needs to be useful. You can hate Excel, but if you're good at it, you'll never be broke. That's what survival looks like.

Boys Learn This. Girls Don't.

Boys are taught early that life is performance-based. From the playground to the pub, they're ruthlessly reminded that failure equals mockery. Miss a goal, you're benched. Show weakness, you're toast. Cry? God help you.

It's brutal, but it's clarifying. Boys learn fast that nobody's handing out gold stars for effort. You're good or you're gone.

Girls, meanwhile, get the full Disney Channel treatment. You're enough. You're special. You're perfect just the way you are. It's all sunshine and vision boards until reality shows up with a bill and zero interest in your "dream to open a healing crystal café."

We don't tell girls the truth. We don't say, "You're not that good at this. Try something else." We don't push them to build skills. We praise the vibe. We reward the attempt. And then we wonder why so many women hit 30 with liberal arts degrees, no savings, and a panic attack every time someone mentions LinkedIn.

The Hypocrisy Industry

Let's talk about the people selling this dream.

The influencers, lifestyle coaches, and fake girlbosses who scream "Do what sets your soul on fire!" from their $2,000 ergonomic chairs—bought with affiliate links and MLM scams. They don't tell you that their real passion is selling *you* a fantasy. That their business model depends on your desperation.

"Passion" is the bait. Your credit card is the switch.

It's rich, really. The same world that pays men for being competent and women for being pretty is also the one whispering in girls' ears, "Just follow your bliss." But only if that bliss involves unpaid internships, overpriced grad school, or starting a blog no one reads. If it doesn't end in debt, it doesn't count.

Passion Doesn't Pay. Skills Do.

We don't need more dreamers. We need more doers. More women who are unromantic about survival. Who pick careers like they pick reliable partners: useful, consistent, and able to contribute something.

Want to change the world? Great. Learn to code. Want to open a bakery? Cool. First, learn profit margins. Want to make art? Amazing. But maybe learn copyright law and digital marketing before you drop $40K on an MFA.

Build the skill first. Let passion follow if it wants to. But if it doesn't? You'll still eat.

The Real Revolution: Raise Competent Girls

If we cared about women's empowerment, we wouldn't just hand them tote bags with glittery affirmations. We'd teach them to build, to fix, to code, to argue, or to invest. We'd train their minds before we praise their hearts.

We'd raise girls who don't need to dream of being rescued—because they're too busy being useful.

We don't need more women chasing passion. We need more women mastering competence, and watching passion chase them.

Men Pick Careers Like Mechanics. Women Pick Careers Like Poets.

Why one group builds empires—and the other builds Pinterest boards.

Let's get one thing straight: men don't need to love their job. They need to beat the job into submission, strap it to the roof, and drag it through life like a trophy kill. That's the default setting. If it pays, it stays. It could be soul-numbing, back-breaking, and completely divorced from any childhood dream. It doesn't matter. If it provides, it's sacred.

A guy could hate accounting more than he hates his mother-in-law's cooking, but if he's good at it and it funds his lifestyle, he'll die at that desk with a spreadsheet open and a Costco hot dog in his gut. This isn't martyrdom. It's strategy. It's competence turned capital. It's "I do this so I don't die broke." No poetry. Just survival.

Why? Because men are taught to pick careers the way mechanics pick tools: Will it get the job done? Can I use it again? Can I charge someone for it?

It's utilitarian. It's emotionless. It's effective.

Women Are Told To Major in Vibes

Meanwhile, women are handed a tote bag full of lies. "Find your passion," they're told. "Choose something that makes your heart sing." Cue the mass exodus into underpaid, oversaturated degrees in *expressing oneself.*

Liberal arts. Sociology. Fashion marketing. Media studies with a minor in "aesthetic theory." Beautiful in theory. Devastating in practice. When the debt collectors come knocking, that "soul-fulfilling" degree doesn't have a payment plan.

No one tells girls, "Study something that will make you indispensable." They're told to study what *feels right.* As if rent accepts emotional resonance. As if job interviews give a damn about "curiosity" or your lifelong obsession with Renaissance textiles.

Men Monetize. Women Romanticize.

A guy will build a plumbing business in a shed and make six figures smelling sewage. A woman will start a handmade candle Etsy store with hopes of passive income and end up crying over supply chain costs and 2-star reviews.

Why? Because men are taught to monetize skills. Women are taught to monetize themselves.

Men are allowed to be boring, practical, and blunt. Women are encouraged to be *inspirational.* As if they're one vision board away from becoming a mogul. It's a dangerous bait-and-switch. One path leads to a pension. The other leads to burnout, MLMs, and calling your podcast a "business."

We Lie About Choice

This is where the hypocrisy becomes a blood sport.

We pretend that women "choose" these soft-skill, low-wage career paths out of pure volition. But that's not true. They're *steered* into them by culture, media, teachers who mean well but don't mention paychecks, and influencers who wouldn't survive a real job interview.

We act like the job market is some neutral buffet where women just happen to go for the cupcakes while men grab the steak. In reality? The girls were told early on that steak was "too aggressive," and besides, cupcakes are prettier. And now they're malnourished, broke, and wondering why their career gives them a stomachache.

Curiosity Is Cute. Cash Flow Is King.

Curiosity doesn't pay the bills. Vibes don't scale. Feelings are not a business model.

You can be the most curious, inspired, well-read barista in the world and still not be able to afford dental. Meanwhile, some guy who grunts his way through HVAC repairs is buying investment properties.

This isn't because men are smarter. It's because men are trained to ask what the world needs, not what their inner child craves. They're taught to think like markets. To identify demand. To build things people will pay for. Women, too often, are told to follow the dream, even when it leads straight into the economic meat grinder.

Fix the Pipeline. Not the Instagram Aesthetic.

If we want to stop watching women get financially wrecked by bad advice, we need to kill the fairy tale. Let them dream, sure—but give them a calculator, too.

Teach them to think like mechanics. Teach them to ask:

- *Does this scale?*
- *Can this feed me in five years?*
- *Will this be in demand during a recession?*

We can romanticize fulfillment after we stabilize income. Nobody ever had a spiritual awakening on an empty stomach. Or at least not one that didn't end in bankruptcy.

Let the poets write. But someone's got to fix the plumbing. And unless you want to be stuck quoting Shakespear to your landlord while begging for an extension, learn the damn trade.

Real Love of the Game Means Playing Any Role

If you ghost when the spotlight fades, you never loved the game—you loved the lighting.

Let's talk sports. Not because we care about them, but because they're the perfect metaphor for commitment—the kind that hurts, humiliates, and still keeps showing up.

A man who loves football and knows he'll never go pro? He sticks around anyway. He becomes a coach, a trainer, a scout, a ref, hell, even a waterboy if it keeps him close to the action. Why? Because he loves the game. Not just scoring. Not just the cheering crowds. The game. The grind. The culture. The strategy. He'll take any position—because the goal isn't fame. It's being useful in the game.

That's real passion. The unglamorous, obsessive kind.

Now switch to the other locker room.

She "Loved" It—Until She Didn't

Many women are told they "love" a sport. Dance, volleyball, gymnastics—whichever one comes with matching outfits and Instagrammable moments. And yeah, they might be good at it. Even great.

But when the starting spot disappears? Or the injuries come in? Or when the varsity dream dies?

They vanish.

No assistant coaching. No weekend refereeing. No trying to build it from the sidelines. Just *poof*—on to the next identity. Maybe yoga. Maybe "travel." Maybe becoming a wellness influencer with #ThrowbackThursdays to the sport she supposedly loved.

That's not love. That's lust. That's flirting with identity and bolting the moment it demands sacrifice.

Obsession Builds Infrastructure. Flirtation Posts Reels.

The brutal truth? You can't build a culture, a system, or a legacy with people who flake the second they don't get MVP.

Systems thrive on people who love the process. Who will scrub floors just to be in the building. Who will volunteer, apprentice, mentor, teach, watch tape, or give back.

That's why men's sports have entire economies around them, even at amateur levels. Guys will argue about 3rd-string draft picks from ten years ago like it's a religion. They *donate* their weekends to coach 10-year-olds in rain-soaked parks. Why? Because they love it more than they love being seen loving it.

That's what obsession looks like. It's not sexy. It's not profitable at first. But it sticks. And it builds empires.

The Female Passion Pipeline: A Revolving Door

Let's not pretend this dynamic is exclusive to sports.

This applies to careers, hobbies, and even activism. Women are often taught to pursue what "feels" right, but not what demands sacrifice. When it stops feeling good? They pivot. Rebrand. Burn the old identity and rise from the ashes with a curated LinkedIn update.

You can't build anything with that. You can *sample* a lot, sure. But you can't scale.

Real love means doing the job nobody sees. Cleaning up the locker room. Reading the boring rulebook. Taking the B-role so someone else can shine.

And this isn't about gender *capacity*—it's about gender *conditioning*. Men are taught to suffer for mastery. Women are taught to quit when the vibes go sour and call it self-care.

Love Without Work Is Just a Mood

Let's be clear: passion is not performance. It's not how much you post. It's how much you bleed for it. How often you show up when nobody's watching. How willing you are to do what's needed—even if it's beneath you.

We worship passion, but we forget its true form is work. And not always the kind that wins trophies. Sometimes it's the work that props up the whole damn system so someone else can win.

And until more women are taught that loving something means serving it, not just benefiting from it, we're going to keep seeing feminine passion as fleeting. Lightweight. Decorative.

If You Won't Play Backup, You Don't Deserve Starter

Here's the bottom line, and it's going to sting:

If you love the game, you stay in the arena—even if you're cleaning the seats.

You don't bail when you're benched. You don't quit when you're outscored. You pivot, adapt, and find another way to contribute.

Because real passion isn't about self-expression.

It's about *utility*.

It's about *endurance*.

It's about doing what the system needs, not what your ego wants.

That's what separates the diehards from the dilettantes.

And until more people—especially women—understand this, we'll keep confusing emotional crushes with actual commitment.

Early Skills Are Economic Ammunition

Your childhood hobbies won't pay rent unless you weaponize them.

Let's cut the fluff: competence is a long con. It's not a lightning bolt of inspiration—it's compound interest. The sooner you start building useful skills, the more dangerous you become. Economically, socially, and politically. And yet, we keep wasting the early years of girlhood telling them to be "nice," "creative," or "themselves."

As if "being yourself" pays off student loans.

Meanwhile, boys are out here getting dragged for losing at Fortnite, pushed to win at chess, and taught to turn hobbies into a hustle. Not because they're smarter, but because they're socialized to compete.

Girls? They're praised for effort. For trying. For being sweet. For making cute earrings on Etsy and journaling their "healing journey."

Here's the cold truth: aesthetic interests are not economic weapons. Unless you level them up.

From Soft Skill to Sharp Edge

It's not about changing what girls enjoy—it's about teaching them to scale it. Because you can either build a business out of your interests, or you can tweet about how capitalism ruined your hobby.

- *She loves cooking?* Great. Teach her to dominate multiple cuisines, cost food by weight, and run a ghost kitchen on Uber Eats.
- *She's the "mom friend"?* Don't just saddle her with emotional labour—channel that compassion into high-skill caregiving, nursing, or clinical therapy. Get her licensed. Get her paid.
- *She won't shut up?* Don't scold her. Train her. Put her in debates. Sales. Law. Negotiation. Teach her how to argue for power, not just attention.

Interest can guide the map. But competence fuels the car.

The Delusion of "Talent Will Out"

You know who believes that if you're good at something, the world will magically reward you? People who've never had to survive.

The job market doesn't reward "potential." It rewards receipts. Skills. Results. People who've put in 10,000 hours *before* they graduate, not while they're figuring themselves out during a six-month trip to Bali.

We tell girls they have time. That they'll figure it out. Meanwhile, the guy who's been fixing bikes since he was 12 is now flipping motorcycles on Facebook Marketplace and putting himself through trade school. Not glamorous. But effective.

Skills Make You Uncancelable

In a world where everyone's a brand, having a skillset is like holding an untraceable weapon. You can't be fired if you don't need a boss. You can't be silenced if you bring irreplaceable value. You can't be "restructured" if you built the damn structure.

This isn't about patriarchal bootstrapping or "leaning in." It's about arming girls with the tools to survive a world that will not love them unconditionally. A world that doesn't care how much they journaled, how spiritual they are, or how "aligned with their values" their major was.

It cares about whether you can do something that someone else will pay for. Period.

The Sooner, the Sharper

If you want to raise a girl who can destroy glass ceilings, teach her to swing a hammer first. Not metaphorically—*literally*. Give her a trade. A code language. A business model. A skill stack.

The world is not kind, but it is predictable.

And in that predictability lies your edge:

Early competence buys long-term freedom.

Early competence funds late-stage passion.

227

Early competence is your get-out-of-panic card.

If you want to give girls hope, give them weapons.

Skill up early. Monetize often. Love comes and goes, but competence is forever.

Competence Makes You Relevant—Even When Youth Doesn't

Your face can open doors. But only your skills can keep them from slamming shut.

Let's just say it: the world runs on looks. Especially for women. We don't have to like it, but pretending it isn't true is delusion in a cute hat.

Pretty privilege is real. Doors open for you. Strangers are nicer. Tips go up. Life is easier. But here's the catch: it's all on a timer. A short one. And when the timer dings, the same system that handed you free drinks and fast lanes will ghost you harder than a guy who "just isn't ready for a relationship."

Because the truth is brutal: beauty expires. Competence doesn't.

You Can't Botox a Skillset

We pump billions into staying young. Creams. Peels. Fillers. Filters. It's a full-time job just to keep up the illusion that your body hasn't started renegotiating with gravity.

But no amount of retinol is going to substitute for knowing how to negotiate a contract, build software, run a courtroom, or lead a company.

You can lose your waistline, but not your welding certification.

Your cheekbones may fade, but your clinical license doesn't.

Your face might age, but your portfolio compounds.

That's the secret nobody tells you in your twenties: skills don't sag.

The Culture of Irrelevance

We raise girls in a culture that teaches them to trade in attention. To make themselves beautiful, charming, and desirable. Not to be respected—but to be wanted. And "wanted" is a currency with terrible inflation. The second your novelty wears off, your perceived value tanks.

It's economic violence dressed as empowerment. Because the moment attention fades, so does power—*unless you've built something else.*

That "something else"?

Competence.

Competence Ages Like Wine. Attention Ages Like Milk.

The beauty of being good at something is that it gets better over time. You stack experience. You build a reputation. You become rare. And in a world drowning in superficiality, depth becomes power.

Want to be sexy at 60? Try being the best in your field.

Want to feel unstoppable at 80? Try being the woman whose brain is still in demand.

No algorithm can replace a mind honed by decades of mastery. No younger model can undercut your price when your skill is irreplaceable.

Competent Women Don't Tolerate Incompetent Men

Here's another side effect of building real, enduring value: your standards change. You stop needing validation. You stop tolerating nonsense. You start holding the room, not just hoping to be liked in it.

You don't beg for a seat at the table, you bring your own chair, invoice in hand.

And perhaps most revolutionary of all: once women stop measuring themselves by attention, they stop measuring *others* that way too. Suddenly, "6' tall, earns

6 figures, has a 6 pack, and a sense of humour" gets replaced with "emotionally literate, solid work ethic, and can hold a conversation without quoting Andrew Tate."

The Long Game Is the Only Game

The real flex isn't being hot at 25.

It's being *needed* at 45.

Respected at 60.

Untouchable at 75.

Because beauty gets likes. Competence gets leverage.

And leverage buys freedom, the only currency that never devalues.

Teach Girls to Be Useful, Not Just Unique

Self-expression is cute. Problem-solving pays.

We've been selling girls a dream—a pastel-colored illusion stitched together with Pinterest quotes and TikTok therapy speak. "Be yourself." "You're special." "Follow your heart." It sounds empowering. Until it bankrupts them.

Because being *unique* is great for a dating profile. But in the real world? Usefulness wins.

The Market Doesn't Care About Your Vibe

Uniqueness without utility is just noise. And the job market is full of unique, broke women with degrees in "finding their truth" and $150K in debt to prove it.

We don't need to kill creativity, we need to equip it. Channel it. Build guardrails around it. Because the world doesn't reward dreams. It rewards solutions.

You want equity? Start with efficacy.

Don't just tell girls they can be anything. Teach them how to build something. Fix something. Sell something. Run something.

Because if all you know how to do is express yourself? Then get in line, 10,000 other people are doing the exact same thing, but louder.

Failure Is a Skill. So Is Grit.

We coddle girls out of discomfort. We rescue them from hard math, hard coaches, and hard truths. Then we act surprised when they freeze the first time something doesn't work out.

Stop. Let them fail. Let them learn. Let them fall and figure out how to get up without applause.

Because handling failure is the difference between surviving life and being shattered by it. And life *will* come swinging.

Teach her that tears are not currency. That struggle is not a signal to quit. That dignity comes from getting better, not from being told she's already enough.

"Following Your Dreams" Should Come With a Warning Label

Here's a dose of reality most girls never hear:

Your dream might suck.

It might be unscalable, unpaid, oversaturated, or just plain boring after a few years.

That doesn't mean you're a failure. It means you have to pivot. That's what grown-ups do. You evolve. You adjust. You get practical. Because sleeping on the floor of your childhood bedroom at 35 while "finding yourself" is not the plot twist empowerment promised.

You want freedom? Learn to be useful in a way that doesn't require someone else to fund your passion.

The Future Belongs to the Competent

Not the quirky. Not the cute. Not the "still figuring it out."

The future belongs to women who can solve hard problems under pressure and don't need a round of applause to do it.

Be weird *and* skilled. Be creative *and* competent. But if you have to choose?

Choose to be useful.

Because usefulness is independence.

And independence is what every dream is made of.

Dreams Don't Die—They Grow Up

Here's the part nobody wants to say out loud:

You can still follow your dreams.

But you'll need a toolbox, not a vision board.

The world doesn't care how inspired you feel. It cares whether you can deliver. And while passion is a spark, competence is the engine. That engine is built in the boring hours. The early mornings. The years no one claps for you. And the job you take because rent is due, not because it aligns with your "authentic self."

We don't need fewer dreamers.

We need tougher ones.

Dreamers who can code. Diagnose. Build. Close. Fix. Sell.

Dreamers who show up, not just *feel* inspired.

The fairy tale was cute when you were five. But you're grown now. And the kingdom needs electricians, engineers, medics, litigators, strategists, and not just more girls with "wanderlust" in their bios and no passports.

So let's raise girls who chase purpose with a plan. Who back their ambition with ability. Who don't just sparkle, they solve.

Because the world doesn't owe you a stage.

But it *will* pay you for being damn good at something.

And that, ironically, is how you earn the freedom to chase every dream you've got.

On your terms. With your name on the door.

A New Movement, Rooted in Reality

It's Not About Turning Back the Clock — It's About Getting Real

This isn't a sermon about "traditional values" or an ode to the days when women vacuumed in high heels and men brought home the bacon with a side of unspoken emotional repression. No one's suggesting a time machine back to the 1950s, where domesticity was destiny and career ambitions got left at the altar. That era was a prison for many women. But what came after, the glittering promises of modern feminism, didn't exactly hand over the keys to freedom either. It handed over a Trojan horse.

Let's talk about the fine print.

You were promised liberation. You got burnout.

You were promised choice. You got to do everything: work a full-time job, raise kids, manage the household, stay fit, stay hot, stay relevant on Instagram, and maybe squeeze in some meditation time if the kids didn't trash the living room.

You were told you could "have it all," but you weren't told the cost: emotional exhaustion, economic instability, and a culture that praises hustle while ignoring mental health. You were sold a fantasy, but billed in real time.

Feminism, in its glossy, PR-friendly form, started sounding less like a rebellion and more like a corporate slogan. "Lean in." "Boss Babe." "You go, girl." As if the answer to structural inequality was better posture and a vision board.

But here's the kicker: while women were being handed inspirational quotes and wine mom merch, the world didn't get easier—it got harder. Housing prices shot up. Wages stagnated. Job security evaporated. And instead of real talk about survival, women got TED Talks about empowerment.

Let's be clear.

The goal here isn't nostalgia. It's clarity.

Feminism promised freedom.

What women need now is function.

Freedom means nothing if you don't know how to wield it. If you're "free" to make any choice, but have no tools to succeed in any of them, is that freedom, or just freedom to fail in more expensive ways?

Because the truth is: feminism is not just lying to women anymore.

It's lying to little girls.

It tells them they're enough just as they are, before they've even done anything. It lets them believe that passion pays, that confidence replaces competence, that the universe will reward vibes instead of value. And when reality hits, it hits hard, and these girls have no armour.

That's not progress.

That's malpractice masquerading as empowerment.

We don't need to go backward. But we desperately need to look around. If modern womanhood is defined by being overworked, underpaid, perpetually anxious, and spiritually unfulfilled, maybe it's time to stop pretending modern feminism is working.

The future doesn't need more glitter. It needs grit.

It needs women equipped not just with dreams, but with strategy.

Not just with passion, but with power rooted in skill, direction, and realism.

This book isn't about turning back the clock.

It's about smashing the broken one on the wall—and building something for women that tells the truth.

We Need Feminism That Includes All Women—Not Just the Loudest Ones

Somewhere along the way, feminism lost the plot.

It used to be a movement. Now it's a marketing department.

Once a battle cry for justice, now a content strategy.

Scroll through Instagram, and you'll see what I mean.

The "new face" of feminism is a filtered woman on a minimalist balcony, sipping matcha in a $300 linen pantsuit, being poetic about "boundaries" and "alignment" while hawking sponsored journals and skincare serums.

That's not the revolution. That's the rebrand.

Meanwhile, real women—billions of them—are out here grinding.

Single moms juggling daycare and double shifts.

Immigrant women scrubbing toilets in AirBnBs they can't afford to rent.

Girls in trade schools being told they're "too butch" or "not ambitious enough" for not wanting to chase corporate titles.

These women don't get podcast interviews.

They don't get press kits or literary agents.

Hell, they barely get acknowledged.

Where is their feminism?

Where is their TED Talk?

Spoiler: there isn't one.

Because somewhere between academia and Instagram, the movement got hijacked by elites, influencers, and Ivy League feminists who turned "empowerment" into a mood board. They're not fighting the system. They're profiting from it.

It used to be that feminism was about kicking the door open for all women. Now it's about securing a seat at the brunch table for a very specific kind of woman.

The kind who speaks fluent therapy-speak.

The kind who can afford a self-care retreat in Bali.

The kind who mistakes personal branding for political action.

Let's be blunt:

If your feminism only shows up for women who look like you, think like you, and tweet like you, it's not feminism

It's clique politics in Spanx.

And while the working-class, blue-collar, trad-leaning, or culturally conservative women get written off as backwards, brainwashed, or boring, feminism keeps hemorrhaging credibility. Why? Because it stopped representing women, and started reflecting a very narrow, very curated demo: urban, liberal, upper-middle-class, college-educated, and usually white.

Irony?

Those are the same gatekeepers they swore they were rebelling against.

If feminism wants a future, it needs a recalibration.

Not more conferences, not more slogans, and sure as hell not more Instagram infographics.

It needs to get back to work. Real work.

The kind that helps women survive, thrive, build, and raise families if they want to.

Because until feminism remembers the women who don't go viral,

It won't matter how loud the rest of them are.

It'll still be whispering where it counts.

True Empowerment Starts With Honesty

Let's clear something up: empowerment isn't a pep talk.

It's not "You go, girl" printed on a coffee mug.

It's not curated captions about healing your inner child or manifesting your CEO era.

Real empowerment doesn't care about your mood board.

It cares about your muscle—mental, emotional, and financial.

Because power, by definition, comes with pressure. It demands pain, failure, sacrifice, and most of all—accountability.

But what modern feminism is peddling to women sounds less like power and more like spiritual sedation.

"You're perfect as you are."

"You deserve the world just for existing."

"You never have to settle."

Nice on a T-shirt.

Disastrous as a life plan.

If empowerment means anything, it means capacity—the ability to act, build, pivot, protect, and persevere.

It means you're not enough yet—but you could be if you're willing to bleed a little.

It's not about vibes. It's about value.

It's not about self-love. It's about self-respect, and not the kind you scream into a ring light while crying over a situationship. The kind you earn by getting up early, grinding, failing, learning, and keeping your word when no one else is looking.

Let's get even more honest:

- Telling women they can't fail isn't kind—it's infantilizing.
- Telling them they don't need men isn't empowering—it's delusional.
- Telling them their value never declines is a marketing pitch designed to sell mascara and bad advice.

True empowerment sounds more like:

- "You're not ready—but you can be. Here's how."

- "You're not entitled to success—but you can earn it."
- "You won't always be chosen—but you can always choose wisely."

Hard truths. Heavy ones.

But better than living in a delusion bubble that pops at 35 with no savings, no support system, and a YouTube algorithm full of breakup coaches.

You want a feminism that men can respect? That's it.

Not because it panders to men, but because it mirrors reality.

The irony? That kind of feminism—the honest, gritty, competence-first kind—is also the kind that would actually help women.

Not just feel better.

Do better.

Because anything else? That's not empowerment.

That's retail therapy in disguise.

The Revolution Isn't Pink—It's Productive

Let's be blunt:

You can't "girlboss" your way out of mediocrity.

And no, your trauma doesn't qualify you for a leadership role.

We've spent the last decade trying to rebrand empowerment as an aesthetic—pastel quotes, curated brunches, and limited-edition water bottles that say *"She believed she could, so she did."*

Cute. Useless.

Meanwhile, the world is burning, the economy is collapsing, and real power is still being brokered in rooms women aren't invited into—because while the revolution was posting selfies, someone else was writing the laws.

Here's the uncomfortable truth:

The future doesn't need more influencers in coordinated loungewear.

It needs competent women—the kind who can fix engines, argue court cases, build companies, lead teams, negotiate deals, de-escalate violence, code machines, or train soldiers.

Not women who perform success for likes.

Women who perform under pressure.

Empowerment isn't a branding strategy. It's a battle strategy.

If your version of feminism needs ring lights, merch, and a Pinterest board to survive, it's not a revolution. It's a product line.

Real equality demands utility.

It's not about who looks empowered—it's about who is.

Not just who gets the mic, but who delivers when it counts.

Because equality was never just about opening doors.

It's about who walks through them ready, with tools, tactics, and teeth.

And the kind of woman you want when the power goes out, the deal falls through, or the system breaks?

She's not journaling about her intentions.

She's already solving the damn problem.

That's the revolution.

And it doesn't come in pink.

It comes in *proficiency*.

The Future Is Earned, Not Manifested

Let's land the plane—without the incense, without the vision board, and definitely without another Instagram reel about "aligning with abundance."

Because here's the brutal truth:

You can sage your apartment all you want, your landlord still wants the rent.

The universe is not your boyfriend.

And no amount of "divine feminine energy" is going to negotiate your raise, build your credit score, or get you out of a toxic job.

We've replaced discipline with delusion.

Action with affirmation.

Sweat with vibes.

And then we wonder why so many women feel broke, burnt out, and betrayed by a brand of feminism that promised them the world, but left them with a tote bag and a vague sense of injustice.

Manifesting didn't fail you. You were just sold a fantasy.

You were told empowerment is a mindset.

But a mindset without skill is just a mood.

And the job market doesn't hire moods.

The real enemy was never just patriarchy.

It was the sugar-coated version of feminism that told you your worth was intrinsic, eternal, and effortless.

No.

Your worth is built.

Earned.

Upgraded—through effort, risk, loss, wins, resilience, and, yes, *reality*.

The good news?

Reality can still be won.

But only if we stop coddling, stop curating, and start cultivating something sharper than confidence: competence.

So here's the new doctrine:

- Less "high-vibe." More high-value.
- Less moon ritual. More market research.
- Less "queen energy." More actual strategy.

Next-wave feminism doesn't need a glow-up.

It needs a gear shift.

Because the future is not a mood.

It's not a manifestation.

It's a fight.

And if we want women to win it?

They need more than mantras.

They need tools.

Women need to stop waiting to be chosen by the universe.

They need to start choosing to build something it can't ignore.

Let's get to work.

THE END

www.ingramcontent.com/pod-product-compliance
Lightning Source LLC
Chambersburg PA
CBHW062126020426
42335CB00013B/1108